THE BREATH OF GOD

LORI LYNNE

Gary, Tonya
Autumn, Cam
To my precious,
precious friends!
I love you dearly!
God bless each one of you!
Lori

The Breath of God
Copyright © 2005 by Lori Felder

Scripture quotations taken from the Amplified® Bible, Copyright © 1954, 1958, 1962, 1964, 1965, 1987 by The Lockman Foundation. Used by permission.

Scripture quotations taken from the New American Standard Bible®, Copyright © 1960, 1962, 1963, 1968,1971, 1972, 1973, 1975, 1977, 1995 by The Lockman Foundation

Scripture taken from the HOLY BIBLE, NEW INTERNATIONAL VERSION®. Copyright ©1973, 1978, 1984 International Bible Society. Used by permission of Zondervan. All rights reserved.

The "NIV" and "New International Version" trademarks are registered in the United States Patent and Trademark Office by International Bible Society. Use of either trademark requires the permission of International Bible Society.

Printed in the United States of America. All rights reserved under International Copyright Law. Contents and/or cover may not be reproduced in whole or in part in any form without the express written consent of the Publisher.
Published by
L.L. Publishing
234 W Bandera #131
Boerne, Texas 78006

ISBN # 0-9722826-0-2

Look for the companion music CD from Robin Lees
BREATHE ON ME

DEDICATION

To Scott, thank you for allowing the world to peek into our past. I love you sweetheart.

To my precious boys Josh and Zach, you two are usually the first things I think about each morning and the last thing I pray for each night. I love and adore you two young men. Forever.

To Mom and Dad, without you there would be no book. I am a direct reflection of your commitment to the Lord and your constant guidance in the ways of Him. I love you two so much, forever.

To Kathy, you are absolutely the most talented woman that I know. I am proud to claim you as my baby sister, and thrilled to brag about the incredible woman that you are. You and your company Rudkin Productions made this project possible. Thank you from the bottom of my heart!

To the rest of my precious family, It would be impossible to relate on paper how important all of you are in my life. I am so grateful for your support and constant encouragement. This book would not have made it to press without the dedication of those that love me, constantly pushing me to complete this project. I love each and every one of you dearly.

To Ms. Peg, I will never forget. When you said, "I believe in you," you proved it. I love you forever too.

ACKNOWLEDGEMENTS

To Robin Lees, my dear friend.

Sometimes in life God sends a special someone that instantly grabs a piece of your heart. When I met you I knew this was a 'forever' friendship. An instant relationship grounded in the shared passion we feel about our Lord. I am so grateful God chose me to be your friend.

Robin you are a constant stream of encouragement to me. So many times I didn't want to meet. I just wanted to forget this project and move on to something else in my life. Your persistence in getting me to meet on Tuesday mornings is the very thing God used to make this project happen. If it weren't for breakfast tacos and coffee every Tuesday, I wouldn't have even tried. Thank you for being so darn determined.

I am addicted to your CD 'Breathe on Me.'

When I asked you to help with this project I had no idea He would create something more powerful than even you or I envisioned. You can feel how passionate for Him you are as you sing. It instantly translates to one's heart.

I am moved when I hear it, and I grow desperate for Him with each song as it is sung.

I love you my friend,

Lori

TABLE OF CONTENTS

CHAPTER 1 .1

CHAPTER 2 7

CHAPTER 3 19

CHAPTER 4 39

CHAPTER 5 47

CHAPTER 6 77

CHAPTER 7 83

CHAPTER 8 97

CHAPTER 9 105

CHAPTER 10 117

CHAPTER 11 139

CHAPTER 12 153

CHAPTER 13 163

CHAPTER 14 177

CHAPTER 15 185

FINAL THOUGHTS 193

CHAPTER ONE

Jump on in; you need to take a ride.

Drive along this steep, winding, seemingly endless asphalt road where the trees grow so thick they create a canopy on this narrow path. Where slowly but methodically you make progress down this Hill Country ranch corridor. It's a rather immense piece of property, even for the Hill Country, and it is nestled somewhere among the outskirts of Boerne, Texas.

Miles of blacktop, hill after hill, curve after curve, you finally arrive. The remoteness of where you stop has a sense of peace, but eerily it has a strange sense of isolation.

The Breath of God

As your eyes begin to adjust to the surroundings turn around. Nestled in the trees way over there, it's nearly hidden; see if you can make it out. It has the shape of an extremely modest home. The quarters look like they have been there many years, like a typical mobile home found on most ranches in the Hill Country. One that is isolated from view, strategically placed to not be seen by those entering the ranch. Hidden as if it has something to be ashamed of, secreted by humiliation. Or by pride?

Grab a chair. Linger here for a while. Watch as a silent observer through one of the thin-paned glass windows of the woman's bedroom.

Maybe you had better watch from the comfort of your car. You notice the air sure feels damp out here. The gray skies seem as if they are about to unleash heaven's fiercest blow. The wind has begun to swirl all around you. There is something unusual about this brewing storm, even for Texas.

Drive up as close as you can get to that window. She can't see out, but you need to see in.

Mesmerized by the moment, watch as the heaviness of the clouded sky makes its transformation into a cloaked, dark, black ominous night. As your eyes adjust to the gloomy end of day, you can begin to make out what seems to be the illumination of a television light coming through the window. It often is overshadowed by the horrendous bouts of lightning crackling all around you.

With every bolt of lightning the wind unleashes and vibrates the solidity of your automobile. The wind is beyond description; it is so different; this wind seems calculating in its intent.

Ssshh. Can you faintly hear the words of the TV? Or can you hear the sobbing intermingled with the misery?

Cowering, shivering and scared senseless. I am a 35 year-old woman, frozen from fear. Every explosive crack of lightning sparks a rumble of thunder impossible to speak over. I have every pillow surrounding me, from the down ones I sleep on to the ones that get vigorously tossed aside every time I crawl into bed. They are the same ones I groan about having to put on the bed each morning, but right now they are serving as a fortress against the storm that is raging.

I grovel below whatever covers I can get my hands on; I grab the remote and turn the volume on the TV up to a level that is ear-shattering. I glance out my small bedroom window frosted over by the humidity of the storm. I wonder, "What is the deal with the wind?" Being raised in Oklahoma I can't help but wonder if this is the prelude to a tornado. But it's early Fall. Still the wind is indescribable.

I can't escape the tempest battle that is taking place in the atmosphere. I also can't escape this raging voice in my head and this demanding request in the most private part of my being.

I am hunkered down, tears pouring down my face desperate for someone to help, desperate for anyone to hear me. I find myself once again... completely, remotely alone. With every hair-splitting crack of lightning, I hear the voice.

With every deep guttural roll of endless thunder, my heart races. It's a profoundly powerful voice and I've heard it before.

I grab my ears and shake my head, begging, "No, please, please no." I knew if I gave in to the pounding voice my life would be over. I knew, somewhere in the recess of my being, tonight was going to be different. Tonight I was going to give in. Tonight I would step over that line and submit to the relentless voice in my head.

Tonight that voice had penetrated the very depths of my soul. That incredibly private part. The part that is nobody's business.

Another deafening crack of lightning rattles the walls of my dimly lit bedroom. The fierce wind is sending thousands of acorns and leaves barreling down on this tiny mobile home.

I feel as if I have an audience out there somewhere. It feels like someone is watching. Waiting. One moment it feels like whatever it is might be for me; the next moment I am convinced it is anything but.

CHAPTER TWO

I was proud to the point of arrogance, determined to the point of defiance, and religious to the point of self-righteous. Perfect description, pathetically disgusting.

I was the precise portrayal of what the world calls a 'good girl.'

> I didn't smoke, never took a drag.
> I didn't drink, never had a sip.
> I NEVER took a drug... EVER.
> I didn't even cuss... much.
> I proclaimed my faith, but lived a lie.

I wonder which is worse in God's eyes?

> A cigarette or the destruction of a marriage?
> A glass of wine or the annihilation of a friend?
> A joint or a secret affair?

My game with God was one that He was determined to win. It was a path of pain I was destined to lose.

I looked good for the camera. But I was rank and rotten on the inside. Most of my secrets were tucked privately away where no one would believe them if they were told.

I could smile and praise the Lord with the best of them. I could 'tsk, tsk, tsk,' the gravest of sinners. I could judge, appraise, gossip about and condemn those I did and didn't approve. My tongue was a master at deception and my heart was as cold as ice - all in love of course. All with my Bible under my armpit. Gag me.

I was miserable, and I made those around me even more miserable. No wonder they were so eager to go.

I somehow wished I could escape this fed-up body of mine. I knew I was going to die. I just didn't know how, and I didn't know when, but I knew it was looming in my future.

I knew my life mocked the God I claimed I served. I knew His Word said don't mock Him... it makes Him mad. I knew He was seriously steamed, and I knew He wanted my full attention. I was scared.

Scared senseless.

This was it. I had known this moment had been coming for weeks. I even told Mom; it feels as if whatever it is, is right here in my ear demanding a response. I reach out for the phone; Mom and Dad live on this ranch too. I need help. My mind shrieks, "Put that down!" I drop the receiver like I have just seared my hand with hot coals. This is real, and I am scared.

The pursuit on the part of the voice has been relentless; it is drowning out my sanity. I can honestly say I feel crazy. I am so terrified I can't call anyone to explain for fear they will think I am insane, but I am convinced I am well on my way.

I feel like I could throw up.

"Pleeaasee leave me alone," I beg. "Please."

I begged and then I did what 'raised right' Christians do. I began the rebuke. I tried rebuking every demon in hell right out of the room. I begged every demon in hell to get the hell out of my room. I marched, I grabbed my

Bible, I proclaimed, I decreed and declared, I cried, I pleaded, I moaned but I knew. I leapt back into bed afraid of what was next.

It reminded me of hearing the footsteps of my daddy coming down the hall when my sister Wendy and I had just been in the battle of our lives with our pillows. When we heard him we just knew we were in trouble, and we knew he wasn't kidding. I still to this day remember his silhouette in the doorway, and his voice that always commanded respect. "Girls?"

Wide eyed I would wait for my sissy sister to speak up and all she would do was dive deeper under the covers. Coward. I could at least squeak out, "Yes?"

I wanted to pull a Wendy on this one.

I wanted to hide under the covers and hope by morning this nightmare would be over.

But when I went under, I'm not kidding, it was like I felt the breath. Still makes me have chills when I think about it. I jolted out from underneath the covers, which is where you found me a few paragraphs earlier. It was in that frantic moment to get out from under those covers, because that feeling was beneath there too that I knew. I just knew.

This agony was no demon. This attack was not from

Satan. This assault was ushered in straight from the throne room of God, and I dreaded it with every fiber of my being.

The contrast was too much for me to bear, the hypocrisy too painful to confront, and the reality of a misspent existence way too agonizing.

I hated me.

Some of you who are reading this have hands that are gripped around the wheel of the car just outside the bedroom window. Knuckles white because you are frozen in your seat and you can't get your fingers to respond to your mind to let go. You are trying to make out the face of the woman in the bedroom, but you know it could just as easily be you. Everyone around you thinks you are a wonderful Christian, but you know you, in that private part. And you can't stand you.

There is such symbolism in that mobile home. Hidden where no one can see it. Placed strategically away from view, from pride and from humiliation. So far back on the ranch only you know that it is there. It's accessible, but only for those you allow to find it. I could always find spiritual cohorts for my sin. Always. I never lacked for having someone to help me violate the Word of God. Never.

Mostly my friends from church.

Sometimes the excitement of the sin would last hours, days, weeks, months and, in my case, years. I never once considered stopping; I never once considered it sin.

I was a master at driving that conviction to the far recesses of my soul and justifying the 'why' of my actions. Facing the ugliness of a life so wrapped up in 'stuff' contrary to the Word of God is like facing a firing squad. There is just no getting out of it; something will hit you.

That mobile home was fragile; it could barely withstand the storm. Vulnerable to the lightning and susceptible to the thunder. And the wind, it was defenseless to the wind, and at the mercy of the power behind the wind.

I sat there in the bed that night, vulnerable, susceptible, defenseless and begging in my heart for mercy. It's a scary thing to be terrified of God. That Scripture, 'Woe to him who strives with his Maker'. I understood that.

To make matters worse, the only light I had on was the TV, the only noise drowning out His relentless barrage was the TV. With one horrific clap of thunder, as if that wasn't scary enough, the whole house became completely black. Not even the hum of the air conditioner or the tick of the clock.

I am now terrified. I am in complete, utter darkness and resounding silence.

What happened next, I will remember like it was yesterday for the rest of my life. As I begin to write this book the tears come right up to the surface as they did seven years ago to the month. I reread my journal this morning (from so many years ago) in preparing for writing this book. This profound event happened October 4, 1997.

I remember clutching my worn-out pillow to my chest, sitting there in utter darkness and complete deafening silence where all I could hear was the wind. The howling, relentless wind.

Truthfully, I wondered, "Is He going to kill me?" I knew I deserved it, I knew I had been such a hypocrite, such a fake. I was the one He rebuked; I was the one He called a pit of vipers. I deserved to die, and truthfully I was afraid He was going to make it happen. With all the courage I could muster, still my defiant little self, I started to yell out into the darkness, "What do You want?" But what came out was that same squeaky cry, when Daddy was in the door. It was pitiful, and it was just a quivering "Yes?" I remember hearing in my heart what sounded like audible heartache, "Lori?"

Just... "Lori?"

My head snapped up off my pillow, with the reality the voice had just called my name and it wasn't bellowing "LORI LYNNE!"

It was... "Lori?"

I remember my head pounding, and my falling beside my bed and my sobbing. Through a breaking heart and buckets of tears, I somehow managed to squeak out a sentence that changed my life.

"You said my name?" "You know my name?"

It wasn't that the sound biblical doctrine that my parents had instilled in me didn't include that God knew my name. But it is one thing to study it, it is one thing to be taught it, but it is another thing entirely different to hear Him call you by it. To realize God Almighty just spoke. And He spoke your name.

It is life-changing.

I expected wrath. I received mercy. I rolled to my back, sitting on the floor beside my bed and stared into a wall that couldn't be 24 inches away. I knew something supernatural was happening, and I was so desperately clinging to the fact He didn't sound mad. I had never understood the mercy seat. I had never understood the presence behind the veil. I had never understood the remarkable, intimate encounter with a God so huge, a Savior so loving and a Spirit so powerful that it would leave you breathless. It would leave you overcome. I didn't understand it, but I experienced it.

I sat there for hours, my bottom screaming to get up because it had long ago gone completely numb. I had gasped for breath between the heaving cries, and finally the heavy breathing had subsided. But I was powerless to move and too awed to change anything.

I sat there forgiven, set free, delivered, renewed, upheld, but most of all overwhelmed by the fact He didn't hate me. Awed by the fact He loved me enough to call me by my name, because He wanted me to look at Him. He had to get me to look at Him. If He had come in wrath, my indignant little self would have justified later why I didn't have to change. But He came to me in mercy, so I had no option but to transform. When He called, "Lori?" and I looked up, not with my physical eyes but with my spiritual eyes, and when I saw mercy, something in me happened. I breathed. I inhaled the mercy of God.

Mercy from the only One who could give me mercy.

My friends, my associates, my sphere of influence whom my sin had impacted and caused some terrible, terrible emotional pain, if they could - they would have demanded my head.

But my Savior just wanted that place; you know that private place, the place that is nobody's business. The only way He can get in there... is if you look at Him.

You know there was something to that wind. It ushered in a change of direction in my life, but it also ushered in tremendous chaos. More about that later.

Same room, same mobile home, same woman. Same circumstances, but a totally different heart. No wonder the Word says, "He sees your heart." If He saw anything else, He would never know you have changed.

The next months were the greatest 'new love' moments of my life. When He says you have left your first love, He is talking about the love that I experienced the months that followed my spiritual CPR. I couldn't get enough of Him. I craved being alone with Him. I threw my clothes out of my tiny closet and set up a prayer room. I dove into the Word and it began to come alive like I had never experienced before. I filled my house with praise and worship music, and I began to write. I really don't like writing. I know that's the irony of this whole deal. Only thing worse to me... is teaching. God has a great sense of humor.

I spent the next months just listening and journaling. I hadn't read that journal in seven years. Yesterday morning when I picked it up and began to read it, I cried most of the way through. Blown away by what God had shown me during those months. Things so important to Him, but things I had forgotten. Things I had forgotten. I sit here and write this and wonder, How? Why? How could I have forgotten what He showed me?

CHAPTER THREE

We are just so human it is sickening. I can honestly say the 'direction' of my life changed forever that day in my mobile home. I began to understand God had a plan for me and He was going to use me.

Dangerous direction for a spiritually immature baby.

I had experienced a dramatic, tangible occurrence with the God of Heaven, and I had been emotionally healed and set free. I was ready to conquer the world for my Jesus. Sound familiar to anyone out there?

I had spent several months in the Word; I had written

repeatedly in my journal, "I know Lord I have to grow, I have to get in your Word." Nearly every day that phrase is in there.

For the next year I read the Word religiously. I had to; I remarried and my new husband moved my two young boys and me to Mexico. Yes, Old Mexico, very Old Mexico.

When we were falling in love it was so easy to tell him I would follow him anywhere, I was so in love with him, and I was so in love with my new precious Jesus. When I said it I meant it, I would go anywhere. And they both held me to my promise.

It was several months into this new 'missionary' lifestyle that I began to eye a little more suspiciously my new-found 'loves.' How can anyone love you as much as they say and yet make you so miserable? (My new husband was in the right camp though. When I would cry that, I was referring to God.) I remember night after night, missing my momma and my dad (who cares that I am now 37). I remember begging God to 'GET ME OUTTA HERE'.

Talk about a new-found confusion! This was not part of the plan God was talking about, surely! It would be impossible for me to reach the world from the bedroom of our home in Mexico. Because I was in no way, shape or form going out of that house on my own.

I became a prisoner of my own design, one of my own preferences. During that time, my heart learned to trust and teach my head to calm down and my tongue to shut up. Finally.

I truthfully had it drilled in my head. Have you ever had one of those times when you couldn't escape the Word of God? The verse you want to ignore, the one you have learned to loathe, keeps popping up? It did for me. I should have received it as mercy, but it seriously irritated me. It wasn't until I got it that God began to change everything.

Lamentations 3:28 *(AMP)*
Let him sit alone uncomplaining and keeping silent (in hope), because God has laid (the yoke) upon him (for his benefit). Let him put his mouth in the dust (in abject recognition of his unworthiness) - there may yet be hope.

The only part of that verse I liked were the last five words... "there may yet be hope." Every other word provoked me.

Alone, uncomplaining, silent, putting my mouth in the dust? Not exactly what I felt like doing.

I looked at Mexico as God's fault. At least that made it easier to grasp than that all this heartache was being caused by my **new** husband.

I hated the part that it was for my benefit. I still get uncomfortable when I flip to that verse.

When I finally got it and gave up, God got me out of there. It literally took a hurricane, but that is another story. My husband says, "He was stretching you." I felt like He was stretching my arms out of their sockets. IT WAS PAINFUL.

Who cares if it was the most precious, charming little tourist town in the heart of Mexico? It wasn't home, and I had never had my umbilical cord cut. And when He did it, I felt like I was hemorrhaging to death.

A little wary, no a lot wary, of what I agree with God I will do from now on. I had this plan you see, and He will just have to try to figure how to help me get there, because I am so not going out of this country EVER again. And that's my final answer.

Kinda makes one of your eyebrows raise, huh? You know that probably was not the right thing to say to GOD ALMIGHTY! And it probably was not the right thing to say to my new husband. But I didn't care now. It's been a year and a half since my 'new love' stage and truthfully, pleasing the two of them wasn't as big of a deal anymore.

[I still had bandaids on some of the wounds that had been inflicted on me by the both of them.]

Beginning to hear some of the same 'defiant, little attitude' seeping back out? Yep, it was making a comeback.

I will spare you most of the details of the next two years. Needless to say, with every day, I moved closer and closer. Not to the Lord, but to the edge.

One week right after Christmas my husband and I had a moment of intense, and I mean intense, fellowship. We had spent several days 'being quiet' and not engaging in conversation. Bottom line - we weren't speaking. Then he dropped a bombshell. And it felt like Hiroshima.

You have got to be kidding Scott? Have you lost your mind? We have three teenage boys living in this house and you are leaving for six months a year? You are going to start doing jail ministry each Sunday, so that leaves me here alone with these three 'run over the mother' boys, 18 days a month without you?

Can you hear the hysteria beginning to build? I think this scenario was worse than Mexico, but at this point I wasn't sure.

We had our twenty, eighteen and sixteen year old sons still in the house. More testosterone in our home than in a fertility lab, and I didn't have the stamina for standing up to them. But that wasn't the biggest heartache.

We had been pursuing a ministry situation that was, at that point in my life, my heartbeat. It meant everything to me. I ate it, I drank it, I thought about it non-stop. It was everything to me. And it was over. Without Scott, I knew it was over.

I had a sickening feeling I was reaping.

I remembered Scott was so sad at having to return home from Mexico, but excited God was going to use him when he got here. I remember how he just trusted that God would do what God intended to do. At that point I was thrilled he found consolation in the fact that God was in control. But I would have never imagined God was setting me up. But He did. There is this principle of sowing and reaping in the Word. It's not in there by accident. It's in there because it is real. It is God's law and He sees to it that it happens. We have so misconstrued that with 'the prosperity doctrine' that we miss the real teaching of the principle. I hope to be able to write someday the principle as I have lived it and as I am just now beginning to understand it. It is what governs your life. Get a hold of that... it is what governs the events of your life. Read it, learn it, and adhere to it. What you sow, that and only that will you reap. Man, I wish I had learned that on that fateful night in my trailer. Just because the Lord shows you mercy doesn't mean He instantly brings you up to speed on the many principles in the Word. He leaves how much you want to know up to you - and up until now, He had let me be. Now He wanted my concentration, and boy, did He get it. I am sure it was, however, not the way He wanted it.

Before our 'intense fellowship' I had just had the flyers printed for the new women's ministry I had started in our home. "Come to our Kick Off, Thursday night, such and such time." We had eighty women crammed in our home. It's tough to stand before 80 women and tell how great God is when you are still reeling from what is happening. The thing that made it so hard was it was God's fault. Scott was going to start going to Nicaragua twice a month for eight days at a time. Nicaragua? He would tell me the Holy Spirit was guiding him; I would remind him the Holy Spirit couldn't possibly be telling him that, because the Holy Spirit is God and GOD MAKES SENSE! THIS DIDN'T.

He kept insisting it was God; I kept demanding it was his stubborn nature. And it just got worse and worse and worse. I rallied my table around me, and he rallied his forces around him and the battle began.

Now get a picture of this, supposedly spiritually mature Christians, leaders in ministry, husband and wife, and we are drawing a line in the sand to see who hears from God? Give me a break. I am mortified at how we handled that YEAR AND A HALF OF HELL.

Needless to say, the women in my life tried to help me through it. They consoled me, comforted me and tried to understand. But I wish one of them had said, "Lori grow up!" You know it's that umbilical cord again. I needed him, and I couldn't bear the thought of him leaving me. I felt such a loss and so rejected. And he blamed it on my God.

The women that rallied around me were such a diverse group. We had the 'seniors,' which consisted of my mom, Ms. Peg and Ms Joann, all staunch Southern Baptists. Then we had the "wonder what we are" group. Then we had the Catholics, and well there is just no other word but we had "the Charismatics." These women scared most of us to death. They ran the Catholics off first rattle out of the cage. I watched them pray with one eye open for about a month. They were fun and cool, and they seemed so exciting. I was blown back by their boldness and truthfully a little intimidated.

After the first meeting the leadership determined how

we should go about discipling all the women who showed up at the function. OK, I had a plan. I am an administrator and delegating the responsibility isn't a problem for me, only because I seriously don't like to do it myself.

If I had just stopped and just listened and, here is a thought, if I had just earnestly prayed that God would help me to lay off my husband and see if God was trying to show me something, I would not have lived a year and a half of hell. I could hear the faint whisper of a voice down inside telling me to teach. I honestly laughed out loud, and said out loud, "You have got to be kidding!" I had failed every test more miserably than the last, and I was in no condition to teach anything other than 'If you see a man... run.'

But I had to pretend to teach when one of the five teachers I had delegated to teach didn't show up. I was sitting at that table with 10 sets of eyes staring at me, waiting on some nugget of truth. All I could think of was, "Are you kidding Lord? This is ridiculous... I told you I can't teach." I shouldn't have been surprised though, everything that seemed to be God's request made absolutely no sense to me.

I then watched some of the ladies and their boldness, and my opinion became confused. Within a month of starting the women's ministry, I had a 'check in my spirit' about what was happening. No, I had more than that; I had 'checks' all over the place. (What they said was the Holy Spirit scared people, hurt people, and ran off people. And they said it was my God.)

At this point if I could have run away I would have - and fast. But I had worked myself into a corner in ministry, and God wasn't letting me out of this.

It was another set-up.

I found this precious little church right down the road. The people there were incredible. They had no idea that my life was in such turmoil, and they were so glad to have us there. I found peace there. I talked to the pastor, who was a young guy, excited about his new position and looking to grow his congregation. I told him I needed to move the women's ministry out of my home and asked if we could please move it to the Sunday School section of the church.

Before we moved there I warned him about the charismatic group. I told him no one would be forced to go to that after the big group broke up, but for the ladies who were turned that way, we provided a place for them to meet too. I explained my position about a 'prayer language' and why I felt like I did. After about three months, the women with the 'gift of charisma' had just about more charisma than any of our little church group could handle. I didn't blame them, and I expected it. When you would walk by their classroom door, when they were praying, it didn't sound spiritual; it sounded scary!

They said it was the Holy Spirit.

They said it was my God.

My pastor who was completely sick of it, decided to lambaste (from the pulpit) what I took extremely personally. He declared how ungodly a prayer language was, how it wasn't in the Word, and how misguided those who prayed that way were. I knew he was talking about the women, but it hurt right to the core of my heart. I knew almost everybody in that congregation knew he was addressing the 'women's group' I led. I was mortified. But I also knew when I was the most vulnerable in my life and I couldn't pray, the Holy Spirit opened a door for me to pour out my heart until it was completely empty. And that was what hurt the worst. The pastor told me the thing I knew was genuine about the Holy Spirit was a complete fraud and I was in sin in even thinking that way. I walked out of there numb. He then emailed me and kicked the ladies out of the church. Maybe we needed to go, especially me for not standing up for the truth, but I wasn't sure what the truth was at that moment. I learned a valuable lesson in all that mess.

God had to have pity on me at that moment. However, I didn't feel it.

My church had rejected me. I was convinced my marriage was over. My husband had just flown off to Africa for two additional weeks, to "see what was going on over there" (driven once again by the Holy Spirit). I had been shoved, slapped across the cheek, and verbally attacked. I had a huge glass of tea thrown in my face, and I still have the stains on my Bible. I had been repeatedly lied to, continually lied about and had more than one person barrage me with "It's all happening because you won't take on Satan." I was called a Jezebel, wicked, demonic and even had some try to cast the demons out of me. I would just stare into space and think, "What else?" When my husband was unreachable in Africa, I received the call my dad had just had a massive heart attack. "He may not make it; it's really, really bad." I adore my daddy, and this was horrible.

And truthfully, those details are the ones I CAN tell and just the beginning. Seriously, it was even so, so, SO much worse.

Well that was it... I thought, "This whole ministry

mess is over; Satan has kicked my little ticked off self right back into real estate." I got back to our women's ministry office, and something had happened with the women that devastated me. Some of the women I had gone to battle to defend, hurt me so bad and they called it God. Again. Once again, they called it God, and once again it involved my money. It was the final nail so to speak, in a never-ending quagmire of exploitation.

At that point I had all the manipulation, consultation, expectation and hearing from everybody else what is God that I could have thrown up. I shut the ministry office down for good and went home.

Where I sat for three months - completely numb.

I was without a church, without a husband most of the time, without the heart of my husband for sure, without a ministry, without most of my friends and without a clue. I just sat there, numb. I pondered all the Holy Spirit stuff I felt like I had had crammed down my throat for the last year and a half, and after a month I came to a conclusion. I didn't want any part of it, nothing. If I could have gotten out of all of it... I would have. But they better not dare tell me they have heard from God for themselves or on my behalf. I am convinced they saw how serious I was in my eyes. I wanted to lash out at God and explain to Him, "A whole lot of His people are CRAZY!"

I was seriously convinced they were all crazy, and I never, ever, evvvvverrrr wanted anything to do with any of them again. Except could He please bring Scott home? I missed him. I didn't want to talk about God with him in any way; I just wanted to hold him. It was sad. It was very, very sad.

I remember sitting beside him on our porch the evening I stopped the women's ministry. Enraged I exclaimed, "Everything you and all these people say is the Holy Spirit hurts me so bad, and what the Holy Spirit is telling me is OPPOSITE of what you say. It can't be God. One of us is wrong. One of us has no clue what the Holy Spirit is. You know, I don't even want to know. Everything I have believed **all my life**, everything I have put my confidence in spiritually, you and your fanatical friends, the women, and our pastor have completely wiped out." Borderline screaming I said, "It's all a fraud and so are all of you. **I just don't believe any of this garbage anymore!**" And just for impact as I walked off, I turned and said, "And I never will!" And I meant it.

Until I turned around and begged God all the way into the house with tears streaming down my face, "I didn't mean it, I didn't mean it." I was terrified I had just committed the 'unpardonable sin.'

I spent January, February and March in hibernation. I waited until Scott went out of town to pick up my Bible. If the Holy Spirit even slightly started to whisper, I would snap back "Leave me alone!" I really meant it, and He would.

Months of pondering and mourning make you realize a lot of stuff. I missed the fellowship of my friends, and how I missed my man. But more than any of that I missed my fellowship with the Lord. I can't say there was an emotional breakthrough. I can't say there was a 'scene' like in the trailer. There wasn't; there was just distance, which brought about healing. Each day I would think back on the last year and try to sort out the real from the fake, try to figure out the spiritual from the hideously ungodly.

Hundreds of people, men and women, had crossed our paths in the last year. Each one had their interpretation of what the 'Holy Spirit' was. I was guilty, too. I had fallen into that game we play as Christians, that if a thought crosses your mind, you have to act on it because that has to be God. Oh my gosh, my friend, that is so, so dangerous. It is a path to disaster - I know because I have been there.

I watched relationships being destroyed, devastating

gut-wrenching heartache to families, and confusion to single moms. I watched one of the most precious women I have ever known run from a group of women crying because of what they told her God was telling them to say. That sounds horrible. It was horrible. But it is happening every day with the children of God. They may not run from your presence sobbing. But when they get home, they may just sit there numb and never darken the door of a body of believers again. I'm not so sure I would have, if I didn't have that night in 1997 forever embedded on my brain.

Over the next months, my heart began to heal. I don't want it to ever completely go away, because I never, ever want to go there again.

There is a song the musical group Point of Grace sings that I had forgotten until I read my journal the other day. I had written about what an impact the words had on me. The song is called "God Forbid." I think it needs to be a spiritual anthem for our day.

I now know why God had me write that. Brother, sister listen to me, please... we have lost our fear of God. We use our relationship as His children to justify our actions; we bathe ourselves in the blood of the cross and claim we are forgiven and we continue to pulverize the Word of

God. We toss around "I believe the Lord is telling me" or "I am sensing the Lord is saying," and we cloak it in the Scripture.

Acts 2:17&18 *(AMP)*
And it shall be in the last days, God says
I will pour forth of My Spirit upon all mankind;
And your sons and your daughters shall prophesy;
And your young men shall see visions;
And your old men shall dream dreams;
Even upon My bondslaves, both men and women,
I will in those days pour forth of My Spirit
And they shall prophesy

That is such a tightrope. Losing balance is inevitable, and landing on your back is extremely painful. Staring straight up into the furrowed brow of God immediately evokes reverential fear.

The Breath of God

The more I know your power, Lord
The more I'm mindful
How casually we speak and sing Your name
How often we have come to You
With no fear or wonder
And called upon You only for what we stand to gain
God forbid, that I find You so familiar
That I think of You as less than who You are
God forbid, that I should speak of You at all
Without a humble reverence in my heart
God forbid
Lord, I often talk about Your love and mercy
How it seems to me Your goodness has no end
It frightens me to think that I could take You for granted
Though You're closer than a brother
You're more than just a friend
You are Father, God Almighty
Lord of Lords, You're King of Kings
Beyond my understanding
No less than everything.
God Forbid

Music by Point of Grace

CHAPTER FOUR

There is a balance, and as the bride we HAVE to find it. We as His children are becoming desensitized and numb. We refuse to do the spiritual homework because we like what we hear, we love what we see, and we all want to hear from God. God created us to 'hear from Him.' Hearing from God doesn't come from someone else. Hearing comes from an intimate, **passionate** relationship with your Creator. Jesus abolished the need for someone else to give you access to your God. His sacrifice opened the door where you can march right in to the throne room and plop yourself down right at the feet of the King. I know it seems impossible.

But it isn't... it's scriptural... and it's real.

> ***Ephesians 3:12*** *(AMP)*
> *In Whom, because of our faith in Him, we dare to have the boldness (courage and confidence) of free access (an unreserved approach to God with freedom and without fear.)*

> ***Ephesians 2:18*** *(AMP)*
> *For it is through Him that we both (whether far off or near) now have an introduction (access) by one (Holy) Spirit to the Father (so that we are able to approach Him).*

Megachurches are exploding with those 'in authority' who hear from God. And they all tell you what He said. It's nonsense. Utter and complete nonsense. But why is it happening? I didn't join a church like that, but I surrounded myself with friends like that, who had surrounded themselves with friends like that, etc. etc. etc. Why? How could I have become so darn deceived?

Because it's exciting and they, truly believing they are hearing from God on everyone's behalf, become extremely, extremely bold. Some to the point you don't dare question what they have spoken. Kind of like the saying "I've said it, therefore it has to be true." If you say something enough, you really will begin to believe it.

As painful as the next sentence is to type, it's in the Word so unfortunately for we women, it has to be true.

2 Timothy 3:6&7 *(AMP)*
For among them are those who worm their way into homes and captivate silly and weak-natured and spiritually dwarfed women, loaded down with (the burden of their) sins (and easily) swayed and led away by various evil desires and seductive impulses. (These weak women will listen to anybody who will teach them); they are forever inquiring and getting information, but are never able to arrive at a recognition and knowledge of the Truth.

When my heart was beginning to heal I watched a woman on TV. I would call it preaching or teaching or ministering, but I am not quite sure what it was. She stood in the front of a huge church and the service was televised. I watched this scene turn into a remake of a 'sci fi' movie.

And she called it God.

She began to receive some kind of telepathic information from what she assured everybody was the 'Holy Spirit' of God. When she sporadically received the information it shocked her like an electric current. She began to speak back to this unseen force some mumbo jumbo as if she understood, so she could begin to tell the audience what God had just spoken to her. Then she, cloaked in white, laid down on the floor and told the audience she was making atonement for them. She was praying for the remission of their sins.

What on God's green earth is going on? This was in a church in America.

I sat on the end of my bed stunned. Tears began to fall down my cheeks as I watched this spectacle. They were tears of gratefulness that God had driven me to the Word. At that moment, the heartache of everything I had gone through made sense. At that moment I knew what God had been orchestrating in the last year and a half of my life. I knew I would do what I could.

I watched as the camera panned the audience. I saw faces that were thrilled, moved, stunned, spastic and somber. I wondered how this moment would impact their lives. I wondered if any of them would ever seek to find out the truth. I recognized me in that audience, not physically, but spiritually. Spiritually deceived.

They are forever inquiring and getting information, but are never able to arrive at a recognition and knowledge of the Truth.

I was so glad those words from 2 Timothy were becoming less and less of me, and it was sooo clear that it had been. But why? For the next several months I forgot about the heartache of the past and just prayed about the why. How on earth did I fall into that, and why on earth couldn't I see it?

I think the key to that sentence is the earth thing. This 'sensing God' movement is man's movement. God's movements don't wreak destruction in the integrity of the Word. I was convinced in my heart, and then I set out to prove it to myself. I had always said 'If it's in the Word I believe it,' and I said that sincerely.

My problem was I believed what they were saying was 'in the Word' was in there and never searched it out for myself.

We slap the 'anointing' on anything from gyrating on the floor in the front of the pulpit to blowing the hair back on someone with whom we don't scripturally agree.

There is a man I know who is convinced his anointing is an anointing of rebuke. Rebuke? He doesn't, **nor did I** even understand the anointing.

In this new quest to 'FINALLY FIGURE OUT WHAT THE WORD SAID' I asked some people I considered incredibly solid to write on paper what they thought the anointing was by Bible standards, not man's.

They wrote what I would have written, but we were wrong.

We have anointing abuse EVERYWHERE.

No wonder the world labels us crazy.

CHAPTER FIVE

This study has been an evolution; one that when I sit back, I am stunned to be a part of. One I would have never guessed could have made such an impact on me and on some of my closest friends. A study that has forever changed how I look at the Holy Spirit. This study is out of the Word. Not twisted or convoluted. Just out of the Word. You can judge for yourself if you choose to believe the Scriptures as they are presented.

If you are like me - desperate to know the truth, desperate to truly hear from God - take the gamble. Dive into this with an open mind, a clear heart and a spirit ready to receive truth.

Let's take the warning He put in the Word and not be counted among them. I want to RIGHTLY DIVIDE the Word.

The Holy Spirit divinely operating in your life will make it possible for you to have revelation into the mystery of God like you have never heard or seen before.

This is an exciting time for the children of God. What Satan has ushered into our churches, we are responsible for. We can stand with or against the doctrine that is preached. You won't know what truth is unless you find it for yourself, and where you find it is in the Word.

The truth is in there; you just have to be looking for it. And you have to persevere to find it.

A small remote story I had read in the Old Testament screamed at me to pursue when I began this journey. One I had written about in the margins of my Bible. One I had noted in my journal **seven** years ago on the 30th of October 1997.

Seven is God's perfect number; it is His number of completion. Hallelujah! There just may be some spiritual significance in the timing of this project for me.

Know that as you begin this journey, I am praying for you. You wouldn't be pursuing this if you were not a

Truth Seeker.

Know *God delights in the hearts of His children who want to know Him in Spirit and in Truth.*

How can you define the Holy Spirit of God? I knew for my own spiritual sanity I had to find the answer. Every display of what others said was the Holy Spirit only confused me. Most of the time it just flat out hurt me. I know I am not the only one who has wondered, "How can the Holy Spirit seem so befuddled?"

How can the 'manifestations' that are attributed to Him - that seem so chaotic, so wild and peculiar - be God? But how can the silence in a church when someone has just praised God through a profoundly powerful song evoke nothing? Just silence. No applause, no "Amen," no "Praise God," just silence.

How can one God be so different, so extreme?

He isn't; we are.

We just label us, and how we respond, as Him and His Spirit. That's how the 14,000 denominations have developed. (o.k., slight exaggeration, but it feels like there are that many) That's why one extreme is labeled the frozen chosen and the other is labeled the charismaniacs. There are hundreds of variations in between those two labels.

But we say we serve the same God, the same Spirit and the same Christ. Usually the division of doctrine comes from one's interpretation of how the Holy Spirit operates within the body of Christ.

I had just had an overdose of extreme interpretations, and I was desperate to know the answer, desperate to know the truth, and I knew I couldn't find it in man. I went to the Word, which is where I would like to take you. Prepare your heart for what you are about to read. Prepare your mind to be open to understanding something you have not been taught.

Let the Holy Spirit of God reveal Himself to you as He has defined Himself, not as man has.

Let's just start with His name. The Holy Spirit.

1. He is Holy
2. He is a Spirit

Holy should be the adjective, with Spirit being the noun. But His Holy is a noun, too. Two distinct nouns. Simple, but not really.

Let's understand what Holy means in the Hebrew and in the Greek. Hebrew is the Old Testament; Greek is the New Testament.

In the Old Testament, in the Hebrew... 'Holy Spirit' as an entity is mentioned only **three times**

>Psalm 51:11
>Isaiah 63:10
>Isaiah 63:11

That's it.

So in the Hebrew, when God used the word Holy in connection with His Spirit, what did He mean?

HOLY - in the Hebrew
The word is <u>qodesh</u>

It means:

1. Sacred thing
2. Sacred place

That's it; holy means sacred thing or place. Seems vague.

So in the Hebrew, God is saying the Holy part of His Spirit is:

1. A sacred thing. A thing has form.
   But He says it's Holy; can Holy have form?
2. A sacred place. A place is a location.
   But He says it's Holy; can Holy have a location?

Remember grammar school? Noun- person, place or thing. Holy is a noun. He says His Holy has a formed location.

Let's see how the New Testament defines Holy.

>HOLY - in the Greek
>The word is <u>hagios</u>

1. Fundamentally signifies "separated"

2. Hagios is more comprehensive... It is characteristically Godlikeness. *(GB Stevens, in Hastings' Bible Dictionary)*

So what does the Word of God say about the HOLY of the HOLY SPIRIT?

The Holy is the **separated godlikeness** in a formed location.

That **Holy** as it pertains to His Spirit is:

A formed location that has separated godlikeness.

Burn that in your brain!

Right now probably most of you are saying "Whaaaat?" Hang in here with me. By the time you get to the end of this chapter, this will be one of the most spiritually eye-opening moments of your life. It was in mine.

Now let's define Spirit.

SPIRIT - in the Hebrew
The word is <u>ruawach</u>

1. Invisible, intangible air
2. Gentle breeze
3. Constant wind, by resemblance of breath
4. To blow
5. To breathe
6. Vital principle

SPIRIT - in the Greek
The word is <u>pneuma</u>

1. Breath of nostrils or mouth
2. Movement of air
3. Vital principle

but it is from the root word *<u>pneo</u>*

1. To breathe hard
2. To blow

Now it was at this point I had information overload and could not for the life of me figure out what I was beginning to get my arms around. But I knew one thing, it didn't sound ANYTHING like what I thought would be God's definition through His Word of what the Holy Spirit meant. Trust me, it will eventually make perfect sense. I think you're about to have a huge dose of 'revelation knowledge.'

Let me explain Spirit. Using the Hebrew and the Greek accurate description: A current of air, blown from a holy location, born from the vital principle of God into man.

> ***John 20:22*** *(AMP)*
> *And having said this,* ***He breathed on them*** *and said to them "Receive the Holy Spirit."*

The **Holy** of His Spirit is where we find the character of His nature; it is there we begin to understand the Spirit God has breathed into us. His Spirit is Holy, His Spirit has form, His Spirit has a location, and His Spirit has distinctiveness. It has 'the separated Godlikeness.'

At this point, please pause and go get your Bible. I don't want there to be even a question in anyone's mind if what I am establishing is true or not. The definitions above are straight from the Hebrew and the Greek meanings from the Word of God.

Revelation 4:5 *(AMP)*
And from the throne proceed flashes of lightning and sounds and peals of thunder. And there were ***SEVEN LAMPS OF FIRE BURNING before the throne,*** *which are the* ***SEVEN SPIRITS OF GOD.***

Revelation 1:4 *(AMP)*
John to the seven assemblies that are in Asia: Grace to you, peace from Him who is and who was and who is to come, and from the ***SEVEN SPIRITS who are before His throne.***

(The amplified Bible refers to the seven Spirits here as the Sevenfold Holy Spirit)

Revelation 3:1 *(AMP)*
He, who has the ***seven Spirits of God,*** *and the seven stars, says this; I know your deeds, that you have a name, that you are alive but you are dead.*

What did God breathe into man? What did Jesus breathe on the disciples? He breathed the Holy, separated but single, Godlikeness into man.

But what is the separated? What is the Godlikeness? I believe it is here we usually all fill in our own blanks. And that is where we have all gone astray. We call it the anointing, our gifts, our fruit. That's not what God calls it.

God defines it. There are **seven lamps of fire burning** before the throne, which are the **seven Spirits of God.**

I didn't say it, God did.

The Holy Spirit is a Sevenfold Spirit.

>HOLY - Old Testament
>**Sacred Thing** - *Lamps...* of burning fire
>**Sacred Place** - *Before...* the Throne of God
>
>HOLY - New Testament
>**Single but separate Godlikeness** - Sevenfold Spirit of God

There are seven. Only seven. Seven very defined, seven clearly distinct Spirits of the Holy Spirit of God. But when we discover them, as God intends them... it is painful. Painful because we have so misunderstood His Spirit, for so long.

That is what this study is about. What are the seven Spirits of the Breath of God? What does our 'anointing' really mean? What really is The Holy Spirit of God?

God Almighty breathes His Spirit into man. The first thing man does when he comes out of his mother's womb is gasp for oxygen. He is desperate for air. The first thing that happens at your 'new birth in Christ' is you breathe in the Breath of God. You breathe in His Spirit, blown in from the Throne Room of God.

What that Breath is comprised of is where we get lost, confused and downright wrong.

Go to the Upper Room in your mind. An event that describes it more accurately than I ever could. The day the Breath of God blew down. The day the impact of the anointing resounded.

> ***Acts 2:2&3***   *(AMP)*
> *When suddenly there came a sound from heaven like the rushing of a **violent tempest blast**, and it filled the whole house in which they were sitting. And there appeared to them **tongues resembling fire**, which were **separated** and distributed and which settled on each one of them.*

God provides the perfect word picture of what transpires with the anointing. Everything in those two verses line up with the Hebrew and the Greek for the Holy Spirit of God. Most of you are going to need to take a deep breath before you read this next line, but the tongues that landed on them weren't different languages. The tongues like blazing fire that separated and distributed were the SEVENFOLD SPIRIT OF THE LIVING GOD.

For those of you saying in your mind, 'I told you they weren't languages,' hold your horses... the Spirit of Might, aligning with the Power of God, gave them the ability to communicate in different speech. What landed on them weren't languages, but what indwelled them made speaking in a foreign language possible, what resulted from their being able to communicate with the foreigners was the Power of God.

The end result was the Power of God. *(There is a deeper teaching on this later)*

OK, I don't know if I can successfully convey what is in my heart but I am going to try. Before the Upper Room experience happens in that Scripture, there had to be something transpire in the heavens. Bear with me and let your imagination take you to a place you may have never even considered. This may not be as it really happened, but it certainly could be.

I know it's close to the description of the throne room of God, because Daniel described what he saw.

Daniel 7:9&10 *(NIV)*
As I looked, thrones were set in place, and the Ancient of Days took His seat.

His clothing was as white as snow; the hair of His head was white like wool. His throne was flaming with fire, and its wheels were all ablaze. A river of fire was flowing, coming out from before Him. Thousands upon thousands attended Him; ten thousand times ten thousand stood before Him. The court was seated, and the books were opened.

Standing off in the distance, you see the glow of brilliant light. As your eyes focus in on the reality of what you are seeing, the images become clearer. You are able to make out the outline of two massive thrones. You can see the silhouette of the one on the right, but the other one just seems to blaze. It's a brilliant, dazzling sensation. The activity all around the area is intense. Movement is everywhere; it's impossible to take it all in. At the base of the glowing thrones are seven colossal torches. All seven blazing with fire. All seven radiating something other than heat. All seven as imperial as the thrones. The torches are casting a glow on the thrones that make them shine at a level unseen by earthly man.

Then the activity around the thrones comes to an immediate halt; all the commotion suddenly retreats. Then it happens. The ground around you, the ground at the base of the torches, and the air around the thrones begins to swirl. The winds begin to rise. The noise level is at a fevered pitch. Just as you think the wind couldn't be any more intense, a deafening blast from the glow of the throne blows the flames of the torches into the atmosphere. It's a hailstorm of fire.

The embers blown into the atmosphere are tongues of blazing fire. The circular swirl from the intense current of air gathers the embers into a vortex, and it travels faster than any mind can comprehend. In an instant it disappears.

Something monumental just happened; you just watched the Breath of God impart the anointing.

Deuteronomy 4:24 *(AMP)*
For our God (is indeed) a consuming fire.

The *anointing*. Since we are *anointed* with the Holy Spirit, what is that? And what does *anointed* mean?

Stop, stop, stop at this point before you go any further. Write down what you think the word anointing means. It's really important; I will show you something about that later on in the chapter.

The 'anointing' is a verb. The anointing is action. Christ was, and we are, anointed with the Holy Spirit. The anointing is not the Holy Spirit. The anointing is the **point of physical contact with God.** It is that union when the Breath of God breathes His Spirit into your soul. **It is the combustion of God's breath and your spirit, the point of Spirit-filled contact with man.**

The Spirit of the Living God just arrived to dwell within you; you are anointed. There are not levels of anointed. If you want the truth, hang with me... it's in there.

> ***John 3:34*** *(AMP)*
> *For since He Whom God has sent speaks the words of God (proclaims God's own message),* ***God does not give Him His Spirit sparingly or by measure,*** *but boundless is the gift God makes of His Spirit.*

You cannot grieve, or quench your anointing. But you can His Spirit.

> ***1Thessalonians 5:19*** *(NAS)*
> *Do not quench the Spirit.*

However the same verse is better stated in the NIV translation, "Do not put out the Spirit's fire."

Which translates... You can't put out the Breath (Spirit), but you can sure put out the Holy. *(more on this later in the study)*

I know this goes against everything most of you have been taught. But please stay with me; the Scriptures are there that will help me prove this. We have just been brainwashed to slap 'it's the anointing' on anything from here to Timbuktu.

If anointing is a verb, why then was Christ called The Anointed One? And if the Holy Spirit is 'the anointing' then why isn't the Holy Spirit called The Anointed One? prophets, priests and kings. All anointed. God's physical contact with man. Then Christ, the Anointed One. God's physical contact with man. The Holy Spirit, the anointing. God's physical contact with man.

When Christ went home to reside beside the Father, God's physical contact with man became the Holy Spirit. **The anointing ushered in the physical contact of God with man.** Whether it be His Christ or His Spirit. Remember, Christ said over and over, if I don't go... He won't come.

God wants **physical** contact with you!

Anointing. What is it?

The Hebrew and Greek definitions aren't nouns, they are action phrases.

ANOINTING in the Hebrew
The word is <u>mashiach</u>

1. To rub
2. To consecrate
3. To set apart for service

ANOINTING in the Greek
The word is <u>chrisma</u>

1. To set apart
2. To smear or rub with oil

Chrisma comes from <u>chrio</u> which means through the idea of contact.

See action. Not a noun. Anointing is an action. Anointing is a verb. Not an entity.

One of the, if not the **only,** Scripture people use to 'qualify' the scale of anointing levels, is the 'double portion of Elisha.'

Let me try to explain that according to the Word. I have had people lay hands on me, prophesy over me and write to me that I have a 'double portion anointing.' I believed it because I wanted to. I believed it because it made me feel like God had singled me out above others and given me more of His Spirit than He had given other people, and someday I could maybe do the things Elisha did. I even bought Elisha books to see what my future could look like if my 'double portion anointing' was really, really true. Give me a break. Just another complete distortion of the truth of God's Word. And I was one of the biggest perpetrators, because it felt soooo good to be soooo special. Talk about a double portion, a double portion of pride, one of the 'Imposter Spirits,' which is a whole other study.

Just a side note. There are seven things God hates. Ironically seven? Seven, and He lists them by name. Pride being one. I would say Satan emulates everything God creates, so he can look and feel like God, and the end result usually produces one of the fruits of the imposter spirits. One of the seven spirits of Satan is pride. Hopefully someday I will get to produce that series too. I've gotten off-track. Now back to Elisha's double portion anointing.

If the 'double portion of his spirit' doesn't mean double like we understand double (twice as much), what does it mean? Let's go to the Word. If you think this is painful to read, or are becoming a little uncomfortable, well, welcome to my world.

Nowhere does it say in Scripture it was a double portion anointing by means of measure. It says a double portion of His Spirit. Prophets, priests and kings were anointed. That means they were 'set apart by God.' The anointing came when they were 'smeared with oil.'

God made physical contact with the world when He 'set apart prophets, priests and kings.' The physical contact of God sealed them for service, set them apart, when they were anointed with oil. They were a foreshadowing of Christ.

They were anointed to:
1. Reveal God to man - Prophets
2. Redeem man to God - Priests
3. Rule - Kings

They were a foreshadowing of Christ.

Elisha was a prophet. He didn't need to be anointed twice. He was anointed once, set apart once, for God to use.

When we understand what each word means, and understand the context, it seems so clear. It makes you wonder why it's been so abused.

'Double Portion of Thy Spirit'

DOUBLE in the Hebrew
The word is <u>sheayim</u>

It means: twofold.
The root means: To duplicate, to fold

Get ready for the next definition.

The Breath of God

PORTION in the Hebrew
The word is <u>pey</u>

It means: **From the mouth, as means of blowing. WOW!**

The root word means: To puff, to blow

Not MORE! Portion doesn't mean more!

SPIRIT in the Hebrew
The word is <u>ruawach</u>

It means:
1. Invisible, intangible air
2. Gentle breeze
3. Constant wind, by resemblance of breath
4. To blow
5. To breathe
6. Vital principle

The 'Spirit' is the Breath of God. His Holy Spirit. The separated Godlikeness of His Character. His Spirit.

The same Spirit we are anointed with. The same Spirit Christ was anointed with.

The Portion doesn't mean an extra measure of. It means the action, the physical contact of God breathing

His Spirit into man, the anointing. I'm not making this up; it really is in the Hebrew.

Does the double mean he received two Holy Spirits? Of course not, but why the double?

The Holy Spirit of God didn't come to reside within man until Christ returned to His Throne. In the Old Testament, the indwelling of the Holy Spirit of God didn't happen. The fruit of the Spirit was basically non-existent. David was a great **anointed** king, and yet he murdered a messenger because he didn't like the message.

Why? Because the Holy Spirit didn't reside **within** him. On the other hand, Elijah was fruit laden. He performed the works of Christ. Think about it. He raised the dead, healed the sick, brought fire from heaven, and fed a woman and her son on absolutely nothing in their country's worst famine. He also spent most of his life in utter solitude. He knew His God. A foreshadowing of Christ. He understood of whom he prophesied; he understood what dwelled upon him. A far cry from most of the other prophets, priests and kings.

The Holy Spirit was alive and well in Elijah, and Elisha saw it, and the nation saw it. That is the two-fold part of the double.

Elisha saw the Power of God at work in Elijah. Elisha wanted the Spirit of God to reside upon him so he could produce the effects of the Power of God around him.

He wanted to breathe in so he could breathe out.

Imagine an 8.5 x 11 piece of paper. Fold it in half. You have created a two-fold document. You have duplicate images side by side. All part of the same paper but different. Double. Still one document, not more, just defined.

Double Portion Spirit
The two-fold physical contact of the Spirit of God

What is the two-fold reason for the Holy Spirit? To create change within us so we can produce the character of Christ to those around us.

Two-fold.

The Double means two-fold, to duplicate. That's it. It is the Holy Spirit's charge to gather His bride and to bring home a family to God. God wants physical contact with man... here and in eternity. Bottom line... God wants a family. One He can touch, and one He can feel.

We receive the Holy Spirit of God to reflect the Christ we believe in, and the God whom we serve. Elisha revealed God to man. It's called evangelism. The Holy

Spirit of God aligned with the Power of God to perform the Work of Christ.

The main purpose of Elisha's mission, which was designed to show forth the Glory of the Almighty, as a God of mercy and salvation, making use of common instruments - mere household vessels- to effect His great and gracious purposes. All this was strikingly evangelical. F.W. Krummacher

All this was strikingly the Mission of Christ.

I don't want this revelation to bring condemnation on anybody. I am confused about how we all get so off-track, but not judgmental about those of US who have been railroaded. Remember I am one of 'thee.' I had no accountability when I would say 'it's the anointing,' because how do you question that? My reason for clarity is not to embarrass or convict.

My reason for clarity is this; when we misuse the definition of the anointing to justify our dealings, we devalue the incredible significance of God wanting to touch us. God wanting to possess us.

It is by an act of His Power, not our worthiness. When we try to validate our worth to God because of our 'anointing,' it then becomes about us and not about Him. We then begin to 'qualify' our anointing level because of 'what we have suffered through' to get it. Pride begins to set in. We begin to believe we are more anointed than others, and that sets us up as spiritually deceived. It's a clever trap of Satan. But it's effective. It looks and feels and sounds like God, but it produces pride.

I hate that dang imposter... sometimes it is so hard to tell the difference.

Let's just all face it. We ALL have a double portion. We all have a two-fold portion. No one is more anointed than anyone else. No one's Spirit is bigger or better than anyone else's. We have been given gifts that are expected to produce fruit. **The *quality* of your fruit is determined by how much time you spend alone at the feet of the Throne, in solitude with your God.** Like Elijah, like Christ.

Here's a shocker; it's not about how much work you do for the kingdom of God. We keep scorecards here on earth of who is and who isn't 'spiritual,' according to what they do. We give great 'glory' to those who seem to 'sacrifice' for the call. God says this:

> ***Jeremiah 9:10*** *(AMP)*
> *But him who glories glory in this:* ***that he understands and knows Me*** *(personally,*

directly discerning and recognizing My character), that I am the Lord, Who practices loving-kindness, judgment, and righteousness in the earth, for in these things I delight, says the Lord.

If God's system of eternal reward was based on only 'working for the kingdom' how would that be fair? Somewhere out there is a single mom working two jobs trying to just put food on the table, but she adores her Creator. Every morning at 4:00 a.m. you can find her on her knees. She spends hours in His presence, and her mind while at work is a fountain of praise. She doesn't have time to work at the local shelter volunteering, she doesn't have the energy to help at church, but she has prioritized her life according to God's Word. She seeks Wisdom first. She knows down deep in that private place, the joy she feels rubs off on others she crosses paths with daily. She knows in her speech others hear how much she adores her Lord. She knows when she falls into bed each night exhausted she can rise before the sun, because her God, her Maker is thrilled to meet her in the morning.

Will her reward be less? The Word says, though often overlooked, her reward will be greater. He sends His Spirit to possess you so you can KNOW Him, not work for Him. We just make it so complicated.

That is what we get so confused about with 'the anointing.' Our gifts and our fruit are not our anointing. Our anointing is the physical contact of God Almighty within us! That's just really incredible. The God of Heaven wants to touch me. It is so hard to fathom that He is out there, watching and waiting just for you to believe, so He can breathe. When He breathes His Spirit into you, He can touch you. God Almighty can touch you; He can feel you. You can KNOW about the God who created you. Are you beginning to get this? He wants to touch you; He's anxiously watching, anticipating the moment... when He will finally be able to touch you!

Think about it. When Christ healed, He touched them. When Christ delivered, He touched them. When Christ restored, He touched them. Christ knew the power of touch. Christ knew how to invoke the Power of God. We are encouraged to lay hands on people when we pray for them. Why? God wants physical contact.

We wonder why we don't see more miracles, more signs and wonders like the Bible speaks about. Is our faith really that much weaker? Did God care more back then about revealing Himself than He does now? Why are most churches today powerless? We wonder why so many Christians are powerless. Why does the emotionalism of the era rule, and why does it seem as if the signs and wonders aren't more genuine and tangible. Because we don't understand the 'Power of God.'

We rely on our 'anointing' to bring restoration, healing and deliverance. Your anointing from God has nothing to do with bringing restoration, healing, and deliverance into the lives of others. Your anointing is personal, between you and God. If it were about your anointing, then it would be about you. The Spirit of I AM that has been breathed into you; now that is a different story. He understands the Power of God. Now if He can just get us to understand.

We confuse the 'Spirit of Might' with the 'Power of God,' and we don't have a clue what the difference is. When we do that we leave out what is defined in the Word as "The Finger of God." The Power of God is at His right hand and we need to 'open our spiritual eyes' to begin to comprehend it.

Look at what you wrote down for your definition of 'the anointing.' Doesn't it mean so much more to you, now that you know that the anointing really means your God wants to touch you?

He is watching you. Every breath, every word, and every movement. He is anticipating the very moment when He can finally seize you for eternity. That, my friend, is incredible! He aches to hold you. He died to embrace you. And He reigns so He can possess you. Your Creator wants to **feel you!**

There is a lot of 'new' in this study and this is just the beginning. It still brings a lump to my throat when I read it. I guess because I have been set free. Set free of believing what I hear and learning to crave the Word of God, not on the surface, but in the deep. And you will come to learn that's the 'Spirit of Understanding.'

CHAPTER SIX

THE SEVENFOLD HOLY SPIRIT OF GOD

The anointing of the Holy Spirit, the physical contact of the Breath of God, blowing a hailstorm of fire from the seven torches into our being. What do those seven torches represent?

What did God say Christ the Anointed One was anointed with?

> ***Isaiah 11:2*** *(AMP)*
> *And the Spirit of the Lord will rest on Him.*
> *The spirit of wisdom and understanding,*
> *The spirit of counsel and strength*
> *The spirit of knowledge and the fear of the Lord.*

That is what Christ was anointed with, and what we are anointed with. It is in this Scripture we find the seven-separated Godlikeness of the Holy Spirit of God.

What are the seven blazing torches?... It's the 'Holy.'

It's the *separate but single Godlikeness. It's the character of God.*

1. Wisdom
2. Understanding
3. Counsel
4. Strength
5. Knowledge
6. Fear of the Lord- Truth
7. Spirit of the Lord - Adoption

That's the Sevenfold Spirit of God. When we look at those character words, what do we think?

Wisdom - *wise in thought, ability to make the right choices*
Understanding - *compassionate, sensitive to other's needs*
Knowledge - *intelligent, book-smart*
Counsel - *ability to give great advice*
Might - *power, force or influence*
Truth - *reality, authenticity*
Adoption - *legal rights*

That's all wonderful, but it just kind of gives you an empty feeling about the Seven Spirits of the Holy Spirit of God. It isn't until we begin to understand God's meaning of those words that makes the Sevenfold Holy Spirit of God give you goose pimples.

What changes the world's definition to God's definition? It is that '**Spirit of**.' Get that. The '**Spirit of**' changes them from 'head issues,' as above, to 'heart issues.' *God breathes into the arena of your heart.* Your heart... your leb. In the Hebrew your heart is defined as your leb. That is your mind, will and emotions - the center of your everything - your heart.

The meanings completely change, when they become events of the heart.

When God's Spirit possesses you, your spirit becomes one with His Spirit, and a new creation is born. It's the dawning of a new heart. One who has the...

Spirit of Wisdom
Desperate Craving

Spirit of Understanding
Passionate Obsession

Spirit of Knowledge
Determined Purpose

Spirit of Counsel
Painful Submission

Spirit of Might
Seized Grip

Spirit of Truth
Manifested Reality

Spirit of Adoption
The Inheritance of I AM

Now that sounds more like it. That's God speak.

At this point I am sure some of you are reading this with a furrowed brow and a gazillion questions. I am sure I would be too. I am going to try to give you an abbreviated version of each one of the Seven Spirits of the Holy Spirit. This book cannot possibly do justice to the study of this matter. That is why there is a detailed study book for each one of the Spirits of the Sevenfold Holy Spirit of God soon to be available at your local bookstore. It is my prayer His Spirit has pricked your heart so that you will want to learn more about Him. That you will begin to see the Scriptures as God intends them. This is truly an exciting mystery in the Word, and it will forever change how you perceive The Spirit of the Living God.

CHAPTER SEVEN

The Spirit of Wisdom

I made reference earlier to a small remote story I had read in the Old Testament when I began this journey. One I had written about in the margins of my Bible. One I had noted in my journal seven years ago on the 30th of October 1997.

It was one that had the exact words of how I felt at that time. I related to this story, but I had no idea this story would be the beginning point of an incredible adventure with my God.

I am so excited to share this with you. Let's see if this story intrigues you like it has me for all these years.

1 Kings 10:1-8, 13 *(AMP)*
When the queen of Sheba heard of (the constant connection of) the fame of Solomon with the name of the Lord, she came to prove him with hard questions (problems and riddles).

She came to Jerusalem with a very great train, with camels bearing spices, very much gold, and precious stones. When she had come to Solomon, she communed with him about all that was on her mind.

Solomon answered all her questions: there was nothing hidden from the king which he failed to explain to her.

When the queen of Sheba had seen all Solomon's wisdom and skill, the house he had built, the food of his table, the seating of his officials, the standing at attention of his servants, their apparel, his cupbearers, his ascent by which he went up to the house of the Lord (or burnt offerings he sacrificed), she was **breathless and overcome**.

She said to the king, It was a true report, I heard in my own land of your acts and sayings and wisdom. I did not believe it until I came and my eyes had seen. Behold the half was not told me. You have added wisdom and goodness exceeding the fame I heard. Happy are your men!

Happy are these your servants who stand continually before you, hearing your wisdom.

King Solomon gave to the queen of Sheba all she wanted, whatever she asked, besides his gifts to her from his royal bounty. So she returned to her own country, she and her servants.

In 1997 I felt like that. I just had my first encounter with The King, and I felt like that... breathless and overcome. But I had no idea this would impact me like it did. I pray this begins to affect you to the level it has me. I pray her story opens your eyes about when God says He has anointed us with the Holy Spirit, that the Spirit of Wisdom helps you begin to understand. I pray that as you begin this journey to a distant land, it will be one you have never experienced before. I pray it becomes one you will never forget.

Imagine the Arabian Desert. The images we see are just as it is. The desolation, the barrenness, the aloneness... the wind. Imagine being a woman, 15 years old, and wanting to travel through there. What would make a young woman want to go there? What would cause such a desperate craving in a woman they call their Queen?

"Your Highness, surely you can't be serious?" "I strongly, strongly urge you to reconsider." He knows he is treading on thin ice, he can see the narrowing of the eyes, and he has come to recognize he is only minutes away from igniting her. "She looks so like her mother," Ashtolio groans to himself. *"I wish so desperately she was still alive. Maybe she could control the tempest spirit within her daughter."*

"My Queen, I have always been a faithful and loyal servant to your family, I would be less than that right now, to your father and your mother, if I didn't counsel you against this. This is extremely dangerous for a caravan of men, but to escort you on a 1400 mile journey across the desert for six months doesn't make any sense! You do realize we will be in a blinding sandstorm for at least two months? You have a kingdom to rule; your country needs you here. You cannot abandon your responsibility and be off pursuing the **rumor** of a man! He's a man! Yes he's a king, quite a king, but he is just a man, my Queen. He is just a king."

"Aagh I detest when she does that, when she smugly smiles and acts as if I didn't say a word." "This is utter nonsense." Still reeling from the news and ready to retreat Ashtolio spins on his heels and recoils to the door. "I bid you good day, my Queen. As if pleading, "Please reconsider... please reconsider?"

"Ashtolio?" Stopping dead in his tracks, he doesn't even turn to look at her, because he knows what is coming. Very firmly she begins, "Ashtolio, your concern never ceases to amaze me. I am so grateful, but I can't calm the passion down within me. I must go." Insisting, she adds, "I must go!" The erect posture of a man bred of authority, droops when she forms the words. He knew this was coming. She has no idea what she is demanding. "Foolish woman" he grimaces. A quick nod and he exits her presence. He knows that tone and she won't be changing her mind. Frustrated and infuriated he still can't help but be a little intrigued himself.

Tonight the breeze is as comforting as the music wafting onto the heavily draped patio of the palace. She is glad for time alone. She wishes she could put her finger on this driving force of desire to encounter this king. It can't be the rumors. "How dare he say 'He's a man.' I know that. I am not going to see a MAN!" "They say he is the wisest man to ever live, they say his God is what makes him that way. We have more gods than Israel will ever have. I would like to challenge his God to ours!"

Still pondering the capacity of her gods, extremely unimpressed by their performance, she can't shake the feeling someone is watching. The music is a soothing retreat for her displaced spirit. As she paces the floor, the cold stones underneath her feet go completely unnoticed, which is quite unlike her. Her mind is fixated on the moment. The moment when she sees this king. "I wonder if he will even receive me? I wonder if I will be making this journey for nothing? I wonder if I should send someone ahead to tell him of our arrival? I will take with us the greatest amount of treasure he has ever seen. Then he would be sure to welcome me. Oh, Ashtolio will be furious!" One can't help but notice the smile out of the corner of her mouth at the thought of adding to Ashtolio's trauma.

She has the most restless nights a queen could imagine. She is pampered with every delicacy possible. But even she can't buy some desperately needed rest. The dreaded impossibility of sleep. "Why on earth can't I get this craving out of my mind? Why is this yearning only growing deeper? It has been three months since I stood up to Ashtolio. They are planning the journey every day. Even I have to admit there are so many more details to attend to than I would ever have anticipated."

"It will be worth it," she hears that over and over again. She hears that in the most private part of her being. Those around her think she has gone completely mad. She is convinced what she is hearing is coming from an unseen force, some voice out there watching, driving her to the extreme.

How could she have possibly known what she was hearing was the voice of Solomon's God?

The voice was without mercy, relentless at every turn, every moment, every daylight and night-time hour. Never letting up, never giving in, never bringing peace. Just resolve to get her to come. Wooing her, so to speak, to a throne and to a king.

Let me introduce you to the Spirit of Wisdom.

It starts with a wooing. A voice in that private part of your being. The place that is nobody's business, except the one who put that private part in you. He created in you a void, so He could fill you.

The Spirit's part... He woos you. Your part... you pursue it. With the intensity of the Queen.

Whatever it takes, whatever the cost, no matter how bad the damage to your reputation. Leave behind what the world has entrusted you with... and go to the voice of the one who is watching. You won't have peace until you pursue it.

That is the Spirit of Wisdom. The desperate craving for an intimate encounter with your King.

He woos, you go... with everything that is in you.

What you receive at the foot of the Throne is the revelation of the Wisdom of God. Standing there you will begin to understand the Wisdom of God! Try to grasp this, friend! Through the Spirit of Wisdom, you will begin to pursue the Wisdom of God!

Where is Wisdom? Beside Him. Pursue the Throne.

Proverbs 8:22,23,30 &31 *(AMP)*
The Lord formed and brought me Wisdom forth at the beginning of His way, before His acts of old.

I Wisdom was inaugurated and ordained from everlasting, from the beginning, before ever the earth existed.

I Wisdom was beside Him *as a master and director of the work: and I was daily His delight, rejoicing before Him always.*

Rejoicing in His inhabited earth and delighting in the sons of men.

Proverbs 9:1 *(AMP)*
*Wisdom has built **her** house; **she** has hewn out **her SEVEN PILLARS**.*

Proverbs 1:23 *(AMP)*
*If you will turn (repent) and give heed to my reproof, behold, I (Wisdom) will **pour out my spirit** upon you, I will make my words known to you.*

> ***Proverbs 4:7*** *(AMP)*
> *The beginning of wisdom is to get Wisdom! For skillful and Godly Wisdom is the principal thing.*
>
> ***Proverbs 2:4*** *(AMP)*
> *If you seek Wisdom as for silver and search for skillful and godly Wisdom as for hidden treasures,*
>
> *Then you will understand the reverent and worshipful fear of the Lord and find the* **knowledge of our omniscient God.**
>
> ***Proverbs 4:5&6*** *(AMP)*
> *Get skillful and godly Wisdom, get understanding (discernment, comprehension, and interpretation): do not forget and do not turn back from the words of my mouth.*
>
> *Forsake not Wisdom and **she** will keep, defend and protect you: love her and **she** will guard you.*

We've been taught Wisdom is Christ. But Wisdom is defined as feminine. God certainly didn't make a mistake when He chose to define Wisdom as feminine. She has been called our sister.

We have been taught a distortion of the following Scripture.

The power of God and the Wisdom of God is Christ.

The Breath of God

> ***1 Corinthians 1:24*** *(NIV)*
> *But to those whom God has called, both Jews and Greeks, Christ the power of God and the wisdom of God.*

I don't want to overwhelm you, but just so you aren't confused about Wisdom. That Scripture really means... The Power of God and The Wisdom of God **created** Christ. It's really clear in the Word, but to do this teaching correctly takes more space than is available in this book. Hopefully someday I can clarify.

> ***Proverbs 1:20*** *(NIV)*
> *Wisdom calls aloud in the street, in the gateways of the city she makes her speech.*

Wisdom cries out for disciples from:

> The High Places
> The crossroads
> The gates
> The streets
> The markets
> The entrances
> The broad roads

Do you hear how God defines the wooing? **She** cries out!

God begs, entreats, pleads for you to seek Him, He guarantees you will find Him.

1 Chronicles 28:10 *(AMP)*
...If you seek Him, He will let you find Him; but if you forsake Him, He will reject you forever.

What does that SEEK mean?

The Hebrew word is *baqash*. It means:

1. To find something that is missing or whose location is unknown

2. To search out by any method, specifically through **worship and prayer**

3. The word is used to describe the seeking of the Lord in a covenant relationship

Other verses in Scripture say pursue Him. PURSUE HIM in the Hebrew is *radap*. It means:

1. To follow after or to pursue **relentlessly and passionately**

Seeking Him isn't a passive prayer. Seeking Him is a covenant commitment to persevere until you find Him. Like the word Baquash… to find something that is missing or whose location is unknown.

I can most relate to the word Baquah's definition of the passion in which the Lord wants us to seek Him. There is no greater fear on earth to a momma than to be unable to find one of her children. To be in a swarming mall or at a crowded football game and lose contact with your child brings instant desperation. Everything halts until you locate your child. The most important thing in your life is out of your reach, and you won't stop until you grasp a hold of their hand, until they are safely in your arms.

I believe that's the intensity of the word 'seek' in the Scriptures as it applies to seeking Him.

To find something that is missing or whose location is unknown, to pursue passionately and relentlessly.

To pursue the Voice of God and be able to reach out to the Hand of God and know that you have just entwined your fingers around the grip of the Power of God... powerful.

The Voice of God reaches out the Hand of God to embrace the child of God, to reveal the Word of God, to bring home the heir of God.

It's a powerful thing to begin to understand the Wisdom of God.

It's a powerful thing to hear the Voice of God and realize it's pursuing you. It's a powerful thing to realize the

Hand of God is reaching for you. It's a powerful thing to realize the child of God is you!

You, my friend, are about to embark on an incredible journey. It's a powerful moment to realize the Spirit of God is stalking you.

CHAPTER EIGHT

The Spirit of Understanding

God is a God of order. Where there is a beginning, there is an end. Where there is a start, there is a process. God says to seek Wisdom first, and there is a reason. The Spirit of Understanding is drawn forth from the pursuit of the Spirit of Wisdom. The Spirit of Understanding is the passion to know the Word of God because you have encountered Him. You have encountered His presence and the experience has left you breathless and overcome. You now are desperate to know Him.

Webster's dictionary defines **understanding** as:

1. To grasp something's nature and significance
2. To perceive something or someone.

3. To know thoroughly by close contact or long experience

UNDERSTANDING in the Hebrew
The root word is <u>biyn</u>

1. To separate mentally
2. To perceive
3. To inform
4. To instruct
5. To discern

How can you discern something's nature?

How can you mentally separate someone's significance?

How do you perceive anything?

By thoroughly being in close contact with or having a long experience with them. How can that happen with God? By being in close contact! By having long experience with the Word of God! How can man know God without being in close contact and knowing what He speaks!

Job 32:8 *(AMP)*
But there is a spirit in man; and the inspiration of the Almighty gives them understanding.

Watch this... what is the Lord saying in this verse?

What is the Almighty's *inspiration*?

The word in the Hebrew is <u>*neshamah*</u> and it means:

1. Blast
2. Wind
3. Vital breath
4. Divine intervention

What is that really saying? The Sevenfold Holy Spirit of God *(the inspiration of the Almighty)* breathed into man's spirit gives him revelation understanding. Understanding to mentally separate His nature and significance, understanding to perceive Him, by close contact and long experience. Understanding to 'Know God.' The Spirit of Understanding. It has been breathed into you! You have been given the capacity to spiritually understand the mysteries and the secrets of God; however, you will never understand them unless you pursue them. The Spirit of Wisdom.

How does one come to 'know Him?' How does someone come to understand someone else? You listen to their heart. How does God say to understand Him? Listen to the words of His heart. Not with your ears! If you want to understand who your God really is, listen with your heart, to His heart. Listen to the Words of His Heart. He put the Words of His heart in His Word. That is why we have His Word, so we can know Him.

> ***Proverbs 2:2*** *(NIV)*
> *Turn your ear to wisdom and apply your heart to understanding.*

> ***Proverbs 1:23*** *(NIV)*
> *If you had responded to My rebuke, I would have poured out My heart to you and made My thoughts known to you.*

> ***Proverbs 4:4*** *(NIV)*
> *He taught me and said "Lay hold of My words with all your heart, keep My commands and you will live, get Wisdom, get understanding."*

> ***Proverbs 4:21*** *(NIV)*
> *My son, pay attention to what I say, listen closely to My words, Do not let them out of your sight, keep them within your heart. Above all else, guard your heart.*

> ***Proverbs 7:3&4*** *(NIV)*
> *Keep My commands and you will live, guard My teachings as the apple of your eye, bind them on your fingers, write them on the tablet of your heart.*

The Spirit of Understanding is spiritually defined as the passionate obsession to know the Word of God, so clearly, so intimately that one can begin to grasp the nature, character and temperament of the Spirit of God... the Heart of God.

The Heart of God is breathed into our leb. Our heart - the center of our everything. That is why there is the desperation in the Word for us to defend our hearts. That is where the Spirit of God operates. That is where you first believed in His Son.

The Spirit of Understanding? It is the passionate obsession to know the Word of God. But it is much deeper than one can even imagine. The integrity of God's Word manifested itself in Christ.

John 1:1 *(AMP)*
In the beginning (before all time) was the Word (Christ) and the Word was with God, and the Word was God Himself.

Hebrews 1:2 *(NIV)*
But in these last days he has spoken to us by His Son

In Matthew 17 verse 5, He implores us to "Listen to Him!"

Listen to His Word, listen to His Son.

The Word says over and over, "Get Wisdom, Get Understanding."

The Spirit of Understanding drives you to the Word so you can begin to open your eyes to I AM. The Spirit of Understanding reveals I AM. Understanding I AM is something you obtain.

The Spirit of Understanding? The **Passionate Obsession** to know the Word of God! The Heart of God and His Son. The Spirit of Understanding drives you to His Word, and to His Son.

CHAPTER NINE

THE SPIRIT OF KNOWLEDGE

Hosea 4:6 *(AMP)*
My people are destroyed because of lack of knowledge.

KNOWLEDGE in the Hebrew
The word is <u>da'ath</u>

1. Intimate knowledge of God
2. To perceive the deep things of God

Webster defines INTIMATE as:

1. One's deepest nature
2. Essential, innermost part
3. A place marked by privacy

4. Very personal private matter
5. Closest of friend or confidant

Ephesians 3:19 (AMP)
*That you may really come to **KNOW** (practically through experience for yourself) the love of Christ, which far surpasses **mere knowledge** (without experience) that you may be filled through all your being unto all the **fullness of God** (may have the richest measure of the divine Presence, and become a body wholly filled and flooded with God Himself!)*

Matthew 13:11&12 (AMP)
*And He replied to them, "To you it has been given to **know** the **secrets and mysteries of the kingdom of heaven,** but to them it has not been given, for whoever has **spiritual knowledge,** to him will more be given and he will be furnished richly so that he will have abundance; but from him who has not, even what he has will be taken away."*

In the Word there are several 'knowings.' There is beginning knowledge, spiritual knowledge and 'revelation knowledge.' There is an outpouring right now of 'rampant revelation knowledge,' with very little emphasis on Knowledge 101 and 102.

The **spiritual knowledge** in the above scripture is the Greek word *epiginosko*. It is the part of the 'revelation knowledge' that is a union so deep, so intimate you begin to understand the secrets and mysteries of the kingdom of God (spiritual knowledge or Spirit of Knowledge).

*Vines Expository Dictionary defines the knowledge this way... A knowledge which perfectly **unites** the subject with the object.*

Revelation part of 'revelation knowledge' is

apokalupsis
It means: an uncovering

An uncovering of what? The knowledge. The epiginosko knowledge, born of the ginosko and the oida knowledge of God. Stay with me.

Ephesians 1:17 *(AMP)*
*For I always pray to the God of our Lord Jesus Christ, the Father of glory, that He may grant you a **spirit of wisdom** and **revelation** (of insight into mysteries and secrets) in the (deep and intimate) **knowledge** of Him.*

Revelation knowledge is not an imagining or a spontaneous thought that crosses your mind. Revelation knowledge is not 'hearing from God' on behalf of someone else so we can tell them what God wants for them. Claiming that as 'revelation knowledge' is a horrible distortion of the truth in the Word of God.

Revelation knowledge, according to the Word of God, is the uncovering of the secrets and the mysteries of God based on a deep intimate union with the Lord. It requires 'a Spirit of Understanding.' Driven by your obsession to know the Word. The Spirit of Understanding produces the Spirit of Knowledge. Bear with me as we look at the truth of the Word.

The end result of the Spirit of Knowledge (spiritual knowledge) produces an effect. The effect it produces is what we are so confused about. The true effect of the Spirit of Knowledge is 'revelation knowledge.' It is a knowledge born of intimate union experience into the deep mysteries and secrets of God. Secrets in the Word. Mysteries in the Word.

When you begin to understand the mysteries of God, the hidden nuggets of truth in the Word, you cannot contain it. Revelation knowledge is **born** out of the Spirit of Knowledge. Spirit of Knowledge is **born** out of the Spirit of Understanding. Spirit of Understanding is **born** out of the Spirit of Wisdom (remember Spirit of Wisdom is first). Could it be that we have barely grasped the concept of 'born again?'

The Spirit of Knowledge is a knowing so deep, it is intimate union based on experience so profound it changes how you perceive the knowledge of God. It is an uncovering of the treasures in the Word, not having been uncovered before or revealed to you previously. What revelation knowledge reveals are the mysteries and secrets of God's Word. Revelation knowledge **reveals God** according to HIS WORD. Not detailed secrets for your neighbor you have heard from God on their behalf.

Let me try to briefly explain. To understand the truth of 'revelation knowledge' we first have to completely understand The Spirit of Knowledge.

In the Word two of the knowings are defined as *ginosko* and *oida*.

There is a big difference between the two.

Ginosko in the Greek means:
1. Beginning knowledge
2. Taking in knowledge
3. Coming to know
4. Recognizing
5. Sense of realization

1 John 2:5 *(NIV)*
But if anyone obeys His word, God's love is truly made complete in him. **This is how we know we are in Him.**

> ***1 John 4:13*** *(NIV)*
> **We know that we live in Him** *and He in us,*
> *because He has given us of His Spirit.*

This is *ginosko* knowing.

Ginosko 'knowing' is a sense of a relationship.

> ***John 8:55*** *(NIV)*
> *Though you do not know Him,* **I know Him.** *If I said I did not, I would be a liar like you,* **but I do know Him** *and keep His word.*

This is *oida* knowing.

Oida 'knowing'- a knowing because you have intimately seen.

Oida in the Greek means:

1. To gaze at with eyes wide open, as at something remarkable
2. Intimacy of beholding
3. Looking closely at
4. To discern clearly
5. To stare at

The difference between the two is:
    Ginosko is the process of knowledge
    Oida is the fullness of knowledge

Remember...

Ephesians 3:19 *(AMP)*
*That you may really come to **KNOW** (practically through experience for yourself) the love of Christ, which far surpasses **mere knowledge** (without experience) that you may be filled through all your being unto all the **fullness of God** (may have the richest measure of the divine Presence, and become a body wholly filled and flooded with God Himself!)*

Ginosko creates the relationship. An understanding between the person 'knowing' and the object 'known.' *Vines Word Study*

Oida is beyond believing. Oida creates an intimate experience, a coming together as one by **seeing**. It results in a life intimately bound together with God.

Ginosko results in the 'saving knowledge' of Christ. Beginning knowledge. Head knowledge.

Oida results in the 'intimate knowledge' of God. Spiritual knowledge. The Spirit of Knowledge is heart knowledge. Beyond believing. A knowing because you have seen.

The Spirit of Knowledge is an intimate **union *experience*** into the very most private, deep parts of the mysteries and the Character of God. The Spirit of Knowledge leaves you breathless, with eyes wide open, because you've just understood something remarkable.

Reread this.

Hosea 4:6 *(AMP)*
My people are destroyed because of lack of knowledge.

Lack of Knowledge. The 'knowledge' here is Da'ath.

It means:

1. Intimate knowledge of God
2. To perceive the deep things of God

We are destroyed because of our lack of the intimate knowledge of God, into the deep things of God.

*What is **intimate?***

1. One's deepest nature
2. Essential, innermost part
3. A place marked by privacy
4. Very personal private matter
5. Closest of friend or confidant

Pray about this. I was guilty of 21st century 'revelation knowledge.' My prayer from the beginning of this book was, "Lord let it begin with me." I was guilty. I believed what I was told, I believed what I experienced, I believed what I said. I was clueless to what the Word says the Truth is about 'revelation knowledge.'

The Word says:

> ***Hosea 4:6*** *(AMP)*
> *My people are destroyed because of lack of knowledge.*

I was nearly spiritually destroyed. Some of you reading this are close. The Holy Spirit has gotten so confusing, so convoluted, and so bizarre that you don't even know what you believe anymore.

We are destroyed because we don't understand God's deepest nature, His essential innermost part. We don't understand the intimate; the place marked by privacy, a very personal, private matter.

Personal, private matter. Between you and God alone. It means perceiving the deep things of God. Understanding the Blood, the Breath, the Water and the Holy.

It means a journey that will take you to a distant land. Where you will encounter a King. One you just have to understand. One you will be frantic to get to know. A breath you will be desperate to take. An unseen voice that won't leave you alone. A Spirit breathing down your neck.

Breathe deep. Breathe with your heart. There is a 'separated godlikeness' stirring in the distance. There is a 'knowing' for you being ushered in from the Throne Room of the King. You just have to diligently persevere to find it.

CHAPTER TEN

THE SPIRIT OF COUNSEL

All of God's people are ordinary people who have been made extraordinary by the purpose He has given them.   Oswald Chambers

Elijah, a great man of God. A man whose anointing has gotten the interest of generations. One man probably embarrassed in the hierarchy of heaven at all the attention. A humble sojourner. A man who just knew how to listen.

He listened, but he listened to only One.

The Counsel of God. The sometimes painful Counsel of God. That's just it... sometimes what God has to say hurts. I had a lady in the Bible study I teach come up to me and try to convince me the teaching I had just conveyed was wrong. Ironically, it was on the New Testament teaching of listening to wrong counsel, and what God says in His Word is true counsel. The message I taught was more than a little painful.

I had conveyed what God says is His counsel. But it had those words in it that most of us don't want to hear.

> ***Revelation 3:18,19*** *(AMP)*
> *Therefore I counsel you to purchase from Me gold refined and tested by fire, that you may be (truly) wealthy, and white clothes to clothe you, and to keep the shame of your nudity from being seen, and salve to put on your eyes, that you may see. Those whom I (dearly and tenderly) love, I tell their faults and convict and convince and reprove and chasten (I discipline and instruct) them. So be enthusiastic and in earnest and burning with zeal and repent (changing your mind and attitude).*

Faults, convict, convince and reprove, chasten, discipline and instruct. Her comment to me was eye-opening. "Don't be condemned, don't be so convicted, but (which meant instead of) be of good cheer, be encouraged!"

I think she misunderstood. It says to be enthusiastic, earnest and burning with zeal and REPENT and CHANGE. Not encouraged because we don't need to feel convicted. Makes you shake your head at what in the world she heard coming out of my mouth?!

There was a lot of truth in that conversation though. We as humans hate pain. And we doubly hate emotional pain. It is so much easier to ignore the warnings, disregard the conviction and overlook the demands to be holy.

We like to move on to the 'happy moments' in the Word. We like to talk and preach about the 'blessings of God,' but fail to remind others and ourselves about the 'Holiness of God.' We have been trained from a whole lot of pulpits that the 'blessings' someone has are without a doubt a blessing from God. You know that person, and he or she is not a nice person. Liar, deceiver, mean, rude and hateful, and that is on a good day. But they are in church, and Sunday after Sunday you see them slip their $20 in the offering plate. They are powerful and rich. You are giving every last penny you can scrape up out the ashtray of your car for the offering. You believe in the totality of God's Word, and a way of holiness has marked your life. You are so broke it's miserable. What is up with this? If that teaching is completely accurate, why has God blessed them so much more than you? Their networking is the only reason they even show up on Sunday.

My friend I have a major dose of 'revelation knowledge' for you. They are blessed, but not by the right god, and God in His Word can prove it.

I hate to say it, but we have put way too much emphasis on the 'prosperity' of God. However, we are now seeing a major shift from the 'prosperity doctrine' teachers to the now famous 'prophetic doctrine' teachers. Which by the way, is in direct violation to the Spirit of Counsel.

There are schools of prophets, prophet classes, prophet strategies, prophetic books and prophetic words changing lives all over our country. It used to be the 'in' thing was prosperity. But their message has now shifted. They have gone from prosperity to prophetic. The prophetic is way, way, way more dangerous. God has a serious stake in the abuse of the prophetic, and He takes the counsel of man quite seriously.

So seriously in the Old Testament, a false prophet was as good as dead. *(Jeremiah 14:13-16)* In Revelation I would be scared to death to be a false prophet. The 'prophetic office' as God has defined it in the Word has more often than not been replaced with the 'prophesy of man's counsel.'

Here is an example, and I could list dozens upon dozens, as I am sure you could too.

A self-proclaimed prophet in our area had a dose of 'prophetic revelation knowledge.' In front of a huge congregation he explained to a young lady that her fiancé was going to be a bald man. Not the man who she was engaged to that had a full head of hair. This of course seriously confused the young lady, who toiled over the possibility - was she missing God? Thankfully she finally decided the prophet was nuts. What happened? In the natural, he was labeled. In the supernatural, he was marked. He was false, and he just made God look petty and wrong. He got his prophetic nose where it didn't belong and abused his perceived gift, if he really had it to begin with, and God takes it very, very seriously. He had better be grateful for grace (like all of us), but because he had set himself up as a prophet, in the Old Testament... it would have been curtains for him. However, according to the New Testament, he's still in big, big trouble. *(Revelation 20:10)*

Therein lies a huge problem of our times, chasing a movement around the earth of the 'prophetic,' because we aren't sure we can hear from God ourselves. We want others to authenticate, substantiate and corroborate what we are to 'do.' We call it '**confirmation**.' You know how I know? You have heard me say it before, "I've been there."

God says:

Psalm 32:8 (NIV)
*I the Lord will instruct you and teach you
in the way you should go, I will counsel
you with My eye upon you.*

Psalm 1:1 (AMP)
*Blessed (happy, fortunate, prosperous, and enviable) is the man who walks and lives not in the **counsel of the ungodly** (following their advice, their plans and purposes), nor stands (submissive and inactive) in the paths where sinners walk, nor sits down (to relax and rest) where the scornful (and the mockers) gather. But his delight and desire are in the **law of the Lord, and on His law (the precepts, the instructions, the teachings of God)** he habitually meditates (ponders and studies) by day and by night.*

New Testament Interpretation of the 'Law of the Lord, and on His law' is ... He **pursues** the Word of God. Do you know what the root word of the 'ungodly' means in the Greek?

1. To be wrong
2. To declare wrong
3. To disturb
4. To violate

If they have ever, ever prophesied wrong, you are 'blessed' if you don't listen to what these 'prophets of our day' say. God calls them ungodly (not of God)!

Deuteronomy 18:21&22 *(NIV)*
You may say to yourselves, "How can we know when a message has not been spoken by the LORD?" If what a prophet proclaims in the name of the LORD does not take place or come true, that is a message the LORD has not spoken. That prophet has spoken presumptuously. Do not be afraid of him.

I have watched people in ministry, so convinced they were 'hearing from God,' change the direction of another person's life or an entire family. I nearly had it happen to me. If you are listening to ANYTHING, OR ANYONE, who is telling you that they are 'hearing from God' or 'sensing God' on your behalf... run. As fast as you can. That is a spirit, but not the Holy Spirit of God. Most often the end result of their 'counsel' will be destruction.

The Spirit of God is comprised of the Spirit of Counsel. The Spirit of Counsel is... God has a plan for you; God has an answer for you. You have to pursue **Him** and **His Word** to find it. Not some prophet.

Don't get me wrong; there is godly counsel. But it is NEVER prefaced by "Thus says the Lord" or anything that even remotely resembles that.

Hebrews 1:1&2 *(NIV)*
In the past *God spoke to our forefathers through the prophets at many times and in various ways,* ***but in these last days He has spoken to us by His Son,*** *whom He appointed heir of all things, and through whom He make the universe.*

Let's think back. What were the jobs of prophets in the Old Testament? **Prophets were anointed to reveal God to man.** They were a foreshadowing of Christ. They were a foreshadowing of evangelism.

How on earth could telling a young woman she is not supposed to marry the man she is in love with (who was a precious Christian man) be a prophetic word from God? Then tell her God says to marry some balding man she doesn't even know? Ironically this prophet was a single, bald man also. How does that reveal God to man? How does that tell of Christ? How does that motivate a life of holiness? Unless God changed the prophet's job description. But I am pretty convinced He didn't.

The insanity **HAS** to stop.

I've watched people prophesied new Suburbans, Hummers, houses, wealth, children, going places they will never go, and doing things they will never do - all cloaked in 'Thus saith the Lord.' Mostly because they knew that was the desire of the person's heart to which they spoke. That is so scary!

I've watched a precious woman prophesied over that she would be a world-renowned musical entertainer. I don't know a whole lot about that, but I'm pretty sure singing isn't her strong suit. But she believed it, and she started speaking it. I know God can do anything, but reality is a powerful thing.

I've watched fear grip a group of people because someone had prophesied bombs were put in a bunch of brightly colored cow statues that adorned the street corners of San Antonio. Complete craziness! They claim what they speak is from God! What if it doesn't happen? What if the Hummer or the Suburban never find their way into your driveway? What happens if you never get that house? What happens if you never get rich? What happens if the child you have been desperate to have never comes?

What if the person who prophesied convinces you it was God talking? What if you believe what they said, and God never makes good on what you think He told you? Who will you be confused about? Who will you be upset with? Please make sure it's the prophet. Don't let someone speak 'false prophetic counsel' on you, and you put your hope in it, and then find out it was never a part of

God's plan to begin with.

What you can trust in is that small hidden voice down deep inside you. What you **can't** trust in is a fleeting thought that passes through your brain or someone claiming to be a prophet. To hear from God, you must know Him. To know Him you must understand Him. To want to understand Him, you have to have encountered Him. To hear from God... seek Wisdom first.

That is why God got so downright mad at false prophets back then, and why He still does to this day. It is cloaked in "Thus saith the Lord," and He didn't even say it!

When what was prophesied doesn't happen, it makes Him look like He isn't good for His Word. Here is the reality... God cares more about the reputation of the integrity of His Word than His name.

Psalm 138:2 (AMP)
For You have exalted above all else Your name and Your Word and You have magnified Your Word above all Your name.

Take that to heart. God cares more about the integrity of His Word, than the integrity of His Name. The integrity of His Word manifested in His Son. If God says it, whatever it is... happens. If man says it, be assured... most often, it won't. Don't listen to man; listen to your heart, your 'leb.'

The place the Spirit of God resides.
The center of your everything.

What God says stands.

***Proverbs 19:21** (AMP)*
There are many devices in a man's heart; nevertheless the Counsel of the Lord will stand.

***Proverbs 3:32** (AMP)*
For the perverse are an abomination (extremely disgusting and detestable) to the Lord; but His confidential communion and secret counsel are with the (uncompromisingly) righteous (those who are upright and in right standing with Him.)

***Psalm 33:11** (AMP)*
The Counsel of the Lord stands forever, the thoughts of His heart to all generations.

***Job 42:1-6** (AMP)*
Then Job said to the Lord, I know that You can do all things, and that no thought or purpose of Yours can be restrained of thwarted. (You said to me) **"Who is this that darkens and obscures COUNSEL (BY WORDS) WITHOUT KNOWLEDGE?** *(He*

> *was talking about his three 'friends', and himself) Therefore (I now see) I have (rashly) uttered what I did not understand, things too wonderful for me, which I did not know. (I had virtually said to You what You have said to me;) Hear, I beseech You, and I will speak; I will demand of You, and You declare to me.* **I had heard of You (only) by the HEARING OF THE EAR, but now my SPIRITUAL EYES SEE YOU.** *Therefore I loathe (my words) and abhor myself and repent in dust and ashes.*

That's the difference. That is the counsel of man versus the Spirit of Counsel. **The Spirit of Counsel is not hearing with the ear, but seeing with the eyes, what has been spoken to your heart by the Voice of God.** A knowing of what you have heard. You cannot clearly distinguish the Voice of God if you have the voices of other opinions.

That is why 'great men of God,' like Elijah and Moses, spent most of their lives alone. Most of their lives were in abject isolation. When they heard, they could respond because there was no question to where the Voice was coming from.

The Holy Spirit of God, makes it possible for you to

hear the Voice of God. To simplify... His Spirit can translate to your heart, the plan and the purpose of God for your life. He doesn't need an intermediary (translator).

His Spirit **IS** the intermediary!

Just food for thought, what disciple ever needed to consult a prophet? When they needed a word of direction, they went to the Source. They got alone with God and they prayed, and they fasted, and they prayed some more. Paul never wanted 'prophetic permission' for anything from any prophet. In fact in Acts he did exactly opposite of what a prophet warned him about. He also reprimanded everybody in the room for trying to change his direction from the Holy Spirit. They were determined to get him to abandon what the Holy Spirit had spoken to his heart. He never sought out permission, nor did anyone else in the New Testament. Why do we?

I am not saying there is not a prophetic office in the Word of God. There is. But it makes sense, and it is not what we are being taught. The prophetic office in the Word is not for delegating 'avenues to pursue.' The prophet's job in the New Testament is the same as the prophet's job in the Old Testament. To point to Christ. Anything other than that... they are a false prophet.

Acts 11:43 *(NIV)*

> ***All the prophets TESTIFY ABOUT HIM*** *that everyone who believes in Him receives forgiveness of sins through His name.*
>
> ***Hebrews 1:1&2*** *(NIV)*
> ***In the past*** *God spoke to our forefathers through the prophets at many times and in various ways,* ***BUT*** *in these last days He* **has spoken to us by His Son,** *whom He appointed heir of all things, and through whom He made the universe.*
>
> ***Revelation 19:10*** *(NAS)*
> *For the TESTIMONY OF JESUS is the* **spirit of prophesy.**

What this verse in Revelation really says in the Greek...

The evidence given of Jesus is the vital principle of the prediction.

That is the litmus test for the prophetic. There is the gift of prophecy, and it is just as it was in the Old Testament, the **Words of God**. The prophet told the words he heard from God.

According to Hebrews, because of the 'manifested reality of the Messiah,' what we hear from God we hear from His Son, who is the Word. The Word of God. The completed manifest of the Word of God.

So what is this 'gift of prophecy' that Paul speaks about? It is rightly dividing the Words of God made possible by the Spirit of God. It is under the 'divine inspiration' of the Holy Spirit that one can interpret the Words of God, the testimony of Jesus, of who He was, of who He is, and who He will become. Based and grounded in the Word. One **CAN** foretell of the future... of Jesus, of the bride, of eternity... based on the Word.

I find it puzzling how confused we are as a whole about the 'gift of prophecy.' There is an entire chapter written on the gift of prophecy. That of all the gifts, it is the most powerful and should be the most sought after. That is why it is a gift. The level of the gift operating in your life is up to you. You can open your gift and place it on a shelf and never use it again. Or you can take it to bed with you, use it first thing in the morning when you awake, and even carry it hidden in your heart.

The gift of prophecy is grounded in the Word of God. No wonder it is prized above all gifts. To be able to speak forth the mysteries and the deep secrets of the Word of God, you must **know** the Word of God, you must pursue the Word of God, and you must treasure and embrace your gift.

The gift of prophesy is the 'speaking forth' revelation

based on the Word of God, founded on the testimony of Jesus.

It is the 'divine inspiration' of **understanding** the written Word **and conveying** what the Holy Spirit has revealed to you in the Word. The 'gift of prophecy' is the response to 'revelation knowledge.' God has just given you an incredible truth in the Word of God, revelation knowledge, made possible by the Spirit of Knowledge. To use your 'gift of prophecy' you must 'speak forth' the truth of the Word as His spirit has revealed it to you. Prophecy is not birthed in your head, nor in your 'spirit;' prophecy is birthed in His Word - the spoken Word of God - into the secrets and the mysteries of His Word.

When Paul was defining the 'gift of prophecy,' there was no written Word. The Word of God was literally being written through Holy Spirit revelation. But we now have the written Word of God, which is Christ.

Hebrews 1:1&2 (NIV)
***In the past** God spoke to our forefathers through the prophets at many times and in various ways, **BUT** in these last days **He has spoken to us by His Son,** whom He appointed heir of all things, and through whom He made the universe.*

Revelation 19:13 (AMP)
*He is clothed with a robe dipped in blood, **and His***

name is called THE WORD OF GOD.

So apply the principle that Jesus Christ is the Word of God

***Revelation 19:10** (NAS)*
*For the **testimony of Jesus** is the*
spirit of prophesy.

The Scripture really says...

The evidence given in the Word of God is the vital principle of prediction.

Please read it again and again. It will forever help you define a false prophet.

We are confused the 'prophetic' is 'hearing from God' in our 'spirit,' therefore that gives us license to abuse the gift. Hearing from God is made possible by the Holy Spirit residing within you - the 'Spirit of Counsel.' Hearing from God is not a '**gift** of the spirit.' Hearing from God is a birthright into His family. Hearing from God is the Spirit of Counsel, not the '**gift** of prophecy.'

The prophetic is speaking forth what the Holy Spirit has just revealed to your heart from **His Word**. Paul said... "I preach one thing... that is Christ (The Word) and Him crucified." If you want to operate in the gift of prophesy, speak forth the Words of God. Speak forth Christ.

The root word to all the prophecy words... prophet, prophesying, prophecy etc. is:

<u>Pro</u> - forth
<u>Phemi</u> - to speak

That's it. To speak forth.

It's what we speak forth that gets us in trouble. Can you imagine what an impact we would have if we spoke forth in the true 'spirit of prophecy?' The evidence given in the Word. The testimony of Jesus Christ. What a great day that would be if we used the Word as a weapon because we truly understood it.

That is why Paul said the 'gift of prophecy' is for the believers. The gift is to encourage and convict, to build up and comfort the church and to mature the bride. Only made possible by the totality of the Word. Not man's opinion of what he thinks he's heard. The 'gift of prophecy' can have an impact on the unbelievers too. Only those filled with the Spirit of God can begin to grasp and reveal to unbelievers the incredible plan, lunged into existence, before the beginning of time. The Messiah Mystery. The testimony of Christ.

If you want to hear from God about something personal, some direction you need in your life... seek Wisdom first. You'll receive the Counsel of God. If you want to help someone else 'hear from God,' show them the way to the Wisdom of God.

God has a Voice, and It cries, implores, begs and entreats you to seek Him. The Voice is the same no matter what the need. The Voice is the One with the answer. God's voice is private, and just between you and Him. He knows your need, and He will tell you how He will meet it. If you want to hear from God, here is one long-term guarantee from God Almighty Himself how to hear from Him.

***Psalm 1:1** (AMP)*
*But his **delight** and **desire** are in the **law of the Lord**, and on His law (the precepts, the instructions, the teachings of God)*
*(THE WORD OF GOD) He habitually **meditates** (ponders and studies) **by day and by night.***

The Holy Spirit of God dwells within you. One of the Sevenfold spirits of the Holy Spirit is The Spirit of Counsel. The Spirit of Counsel gives you the distinct capacity to hear the Voice of God. To know that the Voice you hear is One you can trust, One who has your very best interest in mind. But know along with the Voice comes the intense stare from heaven looking right upon you.

God says:

> **Psalm 32:8** *(NIV)*
> *I the Lord will instruct you and teach you in the way you should go, I will counsel you with* **My eye upon you.**

There are a couple of peculiar verses in the Word and most of us have missed them. God has given a visual of watching you that will probably shock most of you. It shocked me. He knows what is going on with you, because He is watching you. There is a distinct parallel between God watching and speaking.

Food for thought; you are never, ever, ever alone. He sees **every** breath, **every** word, **every** movement. He sees it, and because of your anointing... He **hears** it and He **feels** it. Kind of eerie that Almighty God feels you, huh?

Hearing the Voice is a process; it is one that matures with commitment. It is impossible to respond to a voice you barely recognize, the only way to recognize the voice is to KNOW the One who speaks. To UNDERSTAND the One who speaks, and to have ENCOUNTERED the One who speaks.

The Spirit of Counsel requires you to listen, then

respond. God's requests most often don't fall in line with what our desire for our lives would be. It is learning to obey the Voice that requires a deep understanding of the Spirit of Counsel.

Proverbs 19:21 *(AMP)*
There are many devices in a man's heart; nevertheless the Counsel of the Lord will stand.

Elijah is the man in the Word who understood the 'Spirit of Counsel.' Not because of the miracles that he performed, yet that is a huge part of 'listening' and tapping in to the Power of God. But, that his entire life as recorded in the Word was prefaced by, 'Then the Word of the Lord came to Elijah.'

Think about that. Then the Word of the Lord came to Elijah. Crystal clear communication from the Throne Room of Heaven. So clear, when it was spoken, Elijah leapt into action.

Something that didn't 'just happen.'

CHAPTER ELEVEN

THE SPIRIT OF MIGHT

If it is possible to have a favorite, this one is mine by far. There is something about this one that gives me chills. Something in this chapter created a turning point for me, one that contained so many answers about 'why.' Why don't 'signs and wonders' happen like in the Bible times? Why isn't the Power of God more tangible and more real like back then? If you have ever wondered that, you may be in for a wonderful, burden lifting moment. There is a difference between the Power of God and the Spirit of Might, and I can't wait for you to discover the difference.

1 Peter 3:22 *(AMP)*
Jesus Christ, Who has gone into heaven and is at

*God's right hand, with angels, authorities **AND powers** in submission to Him.*

Luke 1:17 *(AMP)*
*And he will (himself) go before Him in the **spirit AND power** of Elijah, to turn back the hearts of the fathers to the children.*

Acts 10:38 *(AMP)*
*How God anointed Jesus of Nazareth with the **Holy Spirit AND** with **power**.*

1 Thessalonians 1:5 *(AMP)*
*For our gospel did not come to you in word only, but also **in power AND in the Holy Spirit** and with full conviction; just as you know what kind of men we proved to be among you for your sake.*

POWER... *Dunamis*

1. Force
2. Especially miraculous power

Holy Spirit of Might

MIGHT... *Gebuwrah*

1. Powerful
2. Warrior

From the root - <u>Gabar</u>

1. To be strong
2. To prevail
3. To exceed
4. To confirm

When the Holy Spirit latches on with the Power of God... just watch what happens.

Ephesians 3:16 *(AMP)*
*May He grant you out of the rich **treasury of His glory** to be strengthened and reinforced with **mighty power (DUNAMIS)** in the inner man by the **(Holy) Spirit (SPIRIT OF MIGHT)** (Himself indwelling your innermost being and personality).*

You have encountered a God so huge, a Savior so loving and a Spirit that has left you breathless. You have been desperate to understand who your God really is. Not the God of the Bible stories that were told to you in Sunday School. But, who is this God who has become so intimate with you? Who is this who has become one with you?

You are beginning to now understand the magnitude of what dwells within you. You notice your mind is constantly drawn toward heaven, and you can't seem to get enough of the Word. It has happened without you even realizing it, but reading this book is beginning to open your eyes. Something supernatural, beyond your present understanding, has possessed you. Your heart and your mind are beginning to think like they've never thought and felt before. You are starting to respond like you have never responded. You begin to notice a tenderness inside of you, a place easily moved when you think about how truly personal He is to you.

What at first was a curiosity with the Word has now been embedded into your heart. The words jump off the pages when you read them, as if He put them in there just for you. You have read Psalm 91 many times before, but with your new-found love, you are convinced He meant His Word just for you. What had once been consoling words on a page is now a love letter from a Savior that is sealed with His Spirit into your heart.

You wonder if anybody else out there can feel the passion you feel when you read His words. You know you can hear His heart in the prose. With every word that is written you can now hear Him and what He is trying to convey. When you lay down His Word, you've learned to just listen.

And you are convinced you can hear Him; it's that same voice that once was off in the distance. A voice now you can instantly recognize. A voice that is remarkably close, one you are certain if you concentrated you might even be able to read His lips.

You have been to this place where you are right now many times before. Listening intently on what He has to say to you. But this time all you can hear are footsteps, and they are getting closer and closer and closer. Your mind and your heart are beginning to race. His intimacy hasn't been quite this intimate before. You can sense He is nearing, and you wonder what is happening. This place is new to you.

Close your eyes; let your spiritual sight take you to a place you have never ever been.

Before He's just spoken. But now He has waited until your resolve was sincere, your commitment earnest, and your heart tender enough to 'listen.' He's watched, as you have grown desperate to find Him. Sometimes He had to watch through His fingers, anticipating which way you would go.

He has sat in the balcony of heaven waiting for this moment, cheering on your arrival, desperate to make this moment happen for you. Once you arrive here, there is no turning back. Somehow deep within, you know you will forever be different. You will now understand 'many are called, but few are chosen.'

The footsteps have stopped, and you can sense He's in front of you. Go ahead, open your spiritual eyes, both of them, until you can see the hand. It's Him, and He is reaching for you.

Grab it, seize it, and hang on to it with everything that is in you. You are going on a journey, one where you will need the support of your Savior to continue.

This is a grasp like no other, one you at the moment don't understand. You feel the rugged fingers of a carpenter firmly wrapped around your wrist. Lying in the palm of your hand is the reminder of His humanity. It is the wrist of a horrific sacrifice. With eyes mesmerized by the moment, glued to the grip, you see. You see more clearly than you have ever seen. Your mind is quickly transported to a room thousands of years ago, to a question that will be asked until the end of time. "Now do you **really** believe?"

Your answer doesn't require a verbal response. He can tell by the intensity of the way you have seized His scarred wrist that you do. Then the reality of what you hold hits you. He once was only your Savior, but now you see Him as The Son. To cross that line on the ground, the one that separates the Savior from The Son, you need to hang on.

You've needed a Savior to bring you to where you are,

but for the rest of the journey of your life you need to value the enormity that He is His Son. God sent a Savior but brought home His Son. How have you missed it? How have all these years passed by, and you've never understood the impact of the relationship.

You've been drawn by a voice and now led by a grip to a place only for those who are chosen. There has to be a word which is stronger than humbled. Whatever the word - it defines you. It's different than the first encounter you had with Him. That first time the best word to describe you was broken.

This time you can't separate your eyes from the grip. His Spirit has brought you to this summit of understanding, and you don't want to miss one moment. Your mind is reeling from the grip as you become conscious of your surroundings. You are standing in the place you have only read about. The line you stepped over was the last remnant of a veil, which has now eroded over time just for you. This new place is marked by Holy.

The Spirit of God has propelled you to a place where you have seized the right hand of the Son of God. A place where He reached and you grasped. A place that when your hands made contact, a flashback ricocheted off the very fibers of your being. The blood, the horrible sacrifice, the wonders, the miracles, the words, the wisdom, and the resurrection... the reality of Who in his Godlike humanity He was. It's now pale in comparison to who He IS. You now recognize I AM.

Having been captivated by the grip your spiritual eyes elevate, anticipating the impact. You now know you are about to look into the eyes of the very Son of God. He is the Son who has chosen you to come here. His Spirit is the force that has wooed you to arrive. But nothing you have experienced before could impact you like what is about to come.

With each step He leads you closer. With each breath you draw nearer. Not terrified at what is happening, not scared, just stunned, you are led. And then it happens, He reaches His free hand to grasp the hand of His Father, so He can properly introduce you.

Ephesians 2:18 *(AMP)*
*For it is **through Him** that we both (whether far off or near) now have an **introduction** (access) by one (Holy) Spirit to the Father (so that we are able to approach Him).*

And you realize what just introduced you is the Power of God. The Power of God is what has gotten you here.

The Power of God is what is embracing you here, and the Power of God is what is being revealed to you here.

The Power of God is *in* His right hand. The Power of God is *at* His right hand. Two conflicting Scriptures, but not anymore.

You hold the hand of the Power of God, which is a conduit and holds the mighty right Hand of the Power of God. Without the hand that you hold it would be impossible for you to have ever arrived here. Without the force of the Spirit dwelling inside you, it would be impossible to have crossed over the veil.

Let me introduce you to the Spirit of Might. The powerful driving force that propels you to go. The prevailing force that whispers in your ear you can do this. The prevailing force that knows what is ahead if He can just get you to pursue. The voice of a warrior that speaks to your heart what you have just grabbed a hold of is the two-fold Power of God.

The driving force that demands you see as He sees... Open your eyes! The Spirit of Might has latched on to the Power of God. A combustible combination that sets the environment for the supernatural to emerge. A place where healings happen, demons are discarded, and resurrection transpires.

It's where the 'double portion' is grounded.

You see the same image you have had burned in your brain for decades. Only this time there is no wooden cross behind Him. The silhouette of His frame is no different than the last 2000 years. His arms stretched to each side, one clinging to you ever so tightly, and one embracing the grip of His Father. He earned this moment to reveal it to you.

Overwhelmed you drop to your face, and all you can think, all you can feel, all you can taste, and all you can utter is 'Holy.' Just 'Holy.' You know you are at your inauguration of understanding Holy. Holy does have a place, and you're in it.

Miracles happen **only** here. In this place.

The Spirit of Might. What is it? It's the prevailing, driving force where the Spirit of God embraces the child of God to pursue the Son of God to manifest the Will of God made possible by the Power of God. It's the resolve and the skill of a warrior, making the impossible union happen.

Every God-ordained moment of significance in your life has had those five fundamentals working to affect a result. When those five statements line up, it liberates the activity of heaven.

The problem with the equation is not the Spirit, the Son, the Will or the Power. The problem is with the child. God HAS NOT changed. The same miracle-producing God still resides in heaven and still craves the glory. He can't get the glory if His children aren't glory minded.

The lukewarm hearts of His children, caught up in emotion, do not move the Hand of God. It's worth repeating... **The lukewarm hearts of His children, caught up in emotion, do not move the Hand of God.**

The Spirit of Might is what drives you to the Truth. The Spirit of Might is the force that barrels down on your conscious - reminding you your lifestyle is out of line with the Will of God. The Spirit of Might is the warrior of your soul, discerning good from evil, establishing flesh from spirit.

The Will of God is your Savior. The Will of God is the Truth. The Will of God is manifested in Christ. His Son, the One who bought you and brought you to this place. And His Spirit is driven to keep you here. His Spirit is the bold voice in your head, which dives deep into your heart reminding you that you are wrong. The voice that brings the dreaded conviction. His Spirit knows what you have in store for you, if He can just give you a craving for Holy.

Lives that are marked by compromise create an environment marked by mediocrity that results in a powerless child of God.

The Spirit of Might is the driving force. He is the driving force to the Truth and the driving force to the Power. But to reach out to the Hand that is seeking you and to grasp hold of the **Power that is waiting on you...** you have to cross over the pillars of Holy. Powerless children of God are holy-less children of God.

Holiness is not marked by reputation, by prestige or by influence. Holiness is not distinct by congregations. Holiness runs from the rigid, rules and religiosity. Holiness embraces the Truth. The Fear of the Lord is the hatred of evil. The Fear of the Lord Old Testament style is to embrace the grace of the New Testament message, and that is to live for the Truth.

Jesus said "I am the Truth, and the Truth will set you free." Free from the bondage of sin, free for a life marked by holy, free to explore a place you are invited to go. A place our brother Paul says is for the spiritually mature. A place behind a veil, made possible by the Truth, where He lovingly waits for you to arrive.

He waits to embrace the grip of His blood-bought heir,

so He can introduce you to the Power of God. The Power of God ignites the chemistry of miracles.

The Grip, the Blood and the Flames, all three symbols just waiting behind the veil, anticipating and orchestrating the child to understand, so the child will finally come and seize it.

The Breath that drives you to MOVE is the same Breath that entreats you to come. The Spirit of Might is the force behind the grip that pulls you to your feet and propels you to seize what He paid for with His life, what He paid for with His Son.

CHAPTER TWELVE

The Spirit of Truth

It is an intricately woven fabric of color that man could never possibly understand. It's a tapestry sewn by the very hand of God Himself. One that has lasted from before the first breath of man and will still be dynamic throughout eternity.

A vision - one of a man, a Son, a sacrifice and a family. His heart so huge and He was desperate for children. A love so powerful, He would do whatever it would take to bring home His family. This was no weak imagining; this was Power of God vision.

But it depended on just one thing, a Son. One whose sacrifice would be horrific, One whose agony would be like no other, except the suffering of One.

A Son whose last breath brought the deafening thunder of heaven, or could that be the words they used to describe the weeping of a Father?

A bonding beyond description. He was the only One who could possibly understand. This boy was His. This Child grabbed His heartstrings from the moment of His inception. His Son, His precious, prized Son. Now His brutalized Child, His sacrificed Offspring, oh the agony.

However, nothing ravaged His heart more tragically than the call that entered His ears on a day He will never forget. Can't you just hear the piercing anguish? "Father!" You can't ignore the brutal hurt. "Father! Father, have You forgotten me?"

Aaggh, the agony.
The darkest moment in the holiest sanctuary of God.
One forever recorded in the archives of a Book.

A Book nestled right on the lap of a Father. A Father who won't ever 'not remember.' A Book only He meticulously maintains. And don't you ever forget it.

A homecoming that defies description. Not a placid, "welcome home Son," pat on the back. But a jump from your seat, run to your baby embrace that may have lasted through a cycle of seasons. How could He ever let Him go?

The deepest of hugs, a tearful Child glad to be home. Back in the arms of His Father. And He hadn't come home empty handed. He came home with a prize He'd set out to attain, a reward that meant even more to the heart of His Father. He brought home His family. He brought home you. What They suffered through was for you. Get that, how dreadfully desperate They were to have you. Don't look at the others around you, They wanted you.

Friend, understanding this place, this moment of the reunion, you have to be able to grasp holy. You have to comprehend that I AM reigns in holy. Jesus Christ is your Savior, I AM is your inheritance. In this place, He's not just your Savior, but even more vividly He's your Brother. Hear that. Your brother. The Truth.

It's a mind-boggling transition. Reality manifested only by the Spirit of Truth, driven by the Spirit of Might, catapulted into existence by the Spirit of Wisdom. **The One Holy Spirit of God**, One who understands the significance of the evolution.

Every intricate strand of the heart of God, grace, peace, love, truth, kindness, comfort, passion, tenderness, sacrifice, power - your Brother capitalizes. He is Grace.

He is Peace. He is Love. He is Truth. He is Comfort. He is Passion. He is Tenderness. He is Sacrifice. He is Power. God's heart physically manifested in the existence of His Son, your Brother. Makes you really grateful to be related. A joint-heir, the Spirit of Adoption, made possible by the Truth.

The Spirit of Truth is the New Testament translation of the Fear of the Lord in the Old. It's not a contradiction; it's a reality manifested of one of the mysteries of God. Fear of the Lord in the Old is the rigid obedience to the Law. Fear of the Lord in the New is the manifested reality of grace. The Truth. The Truth will set you free, free from what? The Law.

To understand the Spirit of Truth, you first have to understand Truth.

> *The Truth will set you free.*
> *You shall know the Truth.*
>
> *I am the Way, the Truth, and the Life. No one comes to the Father but by Me.*

What does that Truth really mean? Is it Christ? Yes, but not only.

I asked a couple of my friends what they thought these verses meant. I can honestly say when I began this I thought the 'Truth' as presented in the Word, meant the 'saving message of the gospel' and Christ. I never really dwelled on it. I had never been taught on it. So when I asked my friends what their opinion was, I wasn't surprised. They both had completely different answers, and neither one sounded anything like my half-baked definition. I think you might be amazed.

The TRUTH is:

alethos

1. Truly
2. Indeed
3. Surely

Alethos comes from the word *aletheia*.

Vines dictionary defines it more clearly than I could ever explain it.

1. Reality lying at the basis of an appearance
2. The manifested, veritable (intensified) essence of a matter

The Truth.

The 'reality manifested' on the basis of an appearance, intensified by the essence of the matter, which is indeed or surely true.

This is nearly always what the Greek meaning for the word Truth is in the New Testament. There are a few times truth is used, and it is referencing a different situation, but when the Word speaks of Christ as Truth, or the Spirit of Truth, this is the definition of Truth.

The reality manifested on the basis of an appearance, intensified by the essence of the matter, which indeed is true.

The more you dwell on that statement, the more overwhelmed you will become. You will begin to become aware of how intense that spiritual definition defines every principle and every promise breathed from the mouth of God.

Think about this "I am the Way, the Truth and the Life."

I am the Way, the Reality Manifested at the basis of my appearance that is indeed true, and I am Life.

All the hype of His coming in the Old Testament would have remained just that had He not appeared in a dingy manger in some remote barn. But because of the appearance, the reality of the Messiah Manifested, the Old Testament build-up became reality.

Don't stop there. Every word spoken about Him in the Old Testament and New Testament because of His appearance proved indeed true. His appearance in a manger, His appearance to the blind, His appearance on the cross, His appearance in the tomb. What was predicted appeared. It became reality; it became truth.

Let me bring it down to a level we can relate to, a story we all love to tell, about a woman dragged to her judgment, about to be dragged to her death.

Arriving on the scene - Manifested Reality. What He died for, the forgiveness, deliverance, grace, and restoration manifested on the basis of His appearance. To the woman, the reality was intensified by the 'essence of the matter.' Death or Life.

Had He remained in the crowd, He would have watched a woman stoned. But because He knew, He brought Truth when He stepped up beside her. Truth for her situation, truth for the crowd's curiosity, truth for the judgment of the self-righteous, but what He wrote on the ground was the most profound.

I don't know what the crowd saw that day in the dirt, but I know about the Hand that scribed it. Those words weren't just for the men in the circle; those words were a warning shot over the bough to the very demons of hell. I AM had arrived and their dreaded reality had finally manifested.

Apply that to every New Testament happening. Every healing, every deliverance and every restoration. I AM stepped up beside them and intervened. When I AM appears, promises in the Word become manifested reality to the child of God.

The promises of God become Truth.

Three times the Spirit of Truth is mentioned in the New Testament, and the title is so profound. All three are in John, and in all three you can nearly hear the desperation in the words of the Savior, pleading for them to finally understand.

As if a last physical attempt to relate to them the greatness of I AM, the reality of I AM, and the scale of I AM - the enormity that He was **The Son.**

The Spirit of Truth... the testifier. The Witness to the manifested reality of the Power of God. The voice that screams from the words of the page and whispers to the deepest recess of one's heart, of Who He was, of Who He is, and Who He will become.

John 15:26 (AMP)
But when the Comforter comes, Whom I will send to you from the Father, ***the Spirit of Truth*** *Who comes from the Father, He will **testify** regarding Me.*

John 16:13 (AMP)
*But when He, **the Spirit of Truth** comes, He will guide you into all the Truth. For He will not speak His own message but He will tell whatever He hears and He will announce and declare to you the things that are to come.*

TESTIFY in the Greek

The word is <u>*martureo*</u>

It means: To be a witness.

The word comes from Martus which Vines defines as:

One who can or does what he has seen, heard or knows.

The Spirit of Truth, a testifier to the Truth. The manifested reality that was foretold, foreshadowed and fashioned. The Reality was intensified by the essence of the matter in the deep recesses of a grave. Where the Finger of God reached from the Throne Room of God, and He laid His hand on His Son and said "Breathe."

The Breath was there and He heard it, and He screams it from the rooftops if only we would listen.

The Spirit of Truth?

The Testifier of the Manifested Reality.

One that has seen, heard and knows all about I AM.

CHAPTER THIRTEEN

The Spirit of Adoption

I AM.

I AM. Think about it. How enormous is that?

How can we possibly understand the magnitude of I AM, the reality of I AM, the scale of I AM? The enormity of His Son and His Father?

We can't. But The Spirit does. And it is His charge to open our eyes to the actuality.

That 'I AM' is the Jehovah God of the Old Testament and the Sacrificed Lamb of the New. That 'I AM' wasn't spoken on accident. That I AM printed on the pages of your Bible means something. I AM isn't just His title. I

AM is your inheritance.

Let's try to grasp something nearly impossible for our human minds to comprehend. But at least this will be a beginning.

I AM in the Hebrew
The word is <u>hayah</u>

1. To exist
2. To become
3. To bring to pass

I AM in the *Greek*
The word is <u>eimi</u>

It means: I exist - used only when emphatic.

What is He trying to convey?

I EXIST and I will bring to pass what is to become. I became, because I EXIST, so I could bring to pass. I bring to pass what is to become, because I EXIST.

What They bring to pass is for **Their family**.

The same is true of Jehovah God and of His Son.

Read it over and over and over. Until you get it. Until the words make your heart stumble in awe.

The Power of the Father is His Son. The Truth of the Father is His Son. The Will of the Father is His Son. The Grace of the Father is His Son. The Peace of the Father is His Son. The Love, Comfort, Passion of the Father is His Son. The Sacrifice of the Father is His Son. The Heart of the Father is His Son.

The Power of the Son is His Father. The Truth of the Son is His Father. The Will of the Son is His Father. The Grace of the Son is His Father. The Peace of the Son is His Father. The Love, Comfort, Passion of the Son is His Father. The Sacrifice of the Son is His Father. The Heart of the Son is His Father.

The Work of The Father is His Son, The Work of His Son is you. It's worth repeating... The Work of The Father is His Son; the Work of His Son is you, His family.

But notice the transition; get your arms around the combination.

The Power of I AM is yours. The Truth of I AM is yours. The Will of I AM is yours. The Grace of I AM is yours. The Peace of I AM is yours. The Love, Comfort, Passion of I AM is yours. The Sacrifice of I AM is yours. The Heart of I AM is yours. Everything I AM has done or will do is for you. Everything I AM is, is just for you! God Almighty, that is just so incredible. It's for you! You have been genetically altered by His Breath, and the inheritance of I AM is for you!

In Isaiah 41 God defines Himself as He does so often throughout the Word, but it's a passage that grips the very core of the human soul. It is one of the most beautiful chapters on who the 'I AM' really is. In verse 10 He begins:

> *Fear not (there is nothing to fear), for I am with you: do not look around you in terror and be dismayed, for I am your God, I will strengthen and harden you to difficulties, yes, I will help you: yes, I will hold you up and retain you with My (victorious) right hand of rightness and justice. (AMP)*

Just in that verse He defines Himself as:

1. I am your God
2. I am your Strength
3. I am your Helper
4. I am your Upholder
5. I am your Justice

In the following nine verses He goes on defining:

6. I am your Defender
7. I am your Comforter
8. I am your Redeemer

9. I am your Developer
10. I am your Provider
11. I am your Establisher

In verse 10 He tells you, "I will **hold you up and retain you with My (victorious) right hand** of rightness and justice." In verse 13 He again says, "For I the Lord your God **hold your right hand**: I am the Lord, Who says to you, Fear not, I will help you."

What a beautiful word picture of the hand of God that holds your hand. It is a hand of victory, rightness and justice. But as powerful as that image is in your mind, can you hear the whisper of the Almighty? Throughout that chapter He laces it in and out, over and over... "Fear not, fear not, fear not, I still am I AM."

Sssh, listen closely. Does the whisper sound familiar? Peter heard it, when the Hand of God reached down and pulled him to safety from the waves that were about to destroy him. A heartbroken religious leader heard the whisper, and his daughter felt the Hand. This man's baby heard I AM whisper, "Arise."

I AM, sent here by I AM. To strengthen you, to help you, to uphold you, to justify you, to defend, comfort and redeem you. Sound familiar? But mostly, do you hear why

He came? So He could touch you. Grasp a hold of the Hand that is reaching for you. It's a grip that leads home.

I AM wants **His** children home. Your Brother paid for your birthright with His blood. Now it is His Holy Spirit that is the executor of your inheritance, the architect of understanding I AM, the One who interprets distinctly to your soul what is entitled with your heritage.

What does the word adoption really mean?

ADOPTION in the Greek
The word is <u>huiothesia</u>

Huio - a child, a son, kin
Tithemi - to place

Nelsons Bible dictionary defines it:
The word-translated adoption literally means "placing as a son." It is a legal term that expresses the process by which a man brings another person into his family, endowing him with the status and privileges of a biological son or daughter.

Galatians 4:4-5 *(NIV)*
Because you are sons, God sent the Spirit of His Son into our hearts, the Spirit who calls out, "Abba, Father." So you are no longer a slave, but a son: and since you are a son, God has made you also an heir.

> ***Romans 8:14-17*** *(AMP)*
> *For all who are being led by the Spirit of God, these are sons of God. For you have not received a spirit of slavery leading to fear again, but you have received a **spirit of adoption** as sons by which we cry out. "Abba! Father!" The Spirit Himself testifies with our spirit that we are children of God, and if children, heirs also, heirs of God and fellow heirs with Christ, if indeed we suffer with Him so that we may also be glorified with Him.*

The Spirit of Adoption produces the realization of being an heir, and of the inheritance belonging to a child of God. The Spirit of Adoption gives you the confidence to boldly come to the Throne to acquire your inheritance.

> ***Galatians 4:4*** *(NIV)*
> ***Because you are sons**, God sent the Spirit of His Son (Spirit of the Lord) into our hearts.*

The arrival of the Holy Spirit into man is based on one's faith in the saving blood of Jesus Christ and is the guarantee of their salvation.

Because you are sons means because you believed. Because you believed means you received His Spirit. Because His Breath resides within you, you are His genetically altered heir.

Once you believe, His Spirit sets about to convince you of who you now **really** are and to produce a realization in your spirit you are a joint heir, a child of God. It's a big job.

Problem is we rarely feel worthy, because we aren't. But His Son paid a big price, and when we don't understand our inheritance it makes His suffering on the cross somehow diluted.

Remember back in this book when you grasped the hand of your Savior, and you crossed over a line? Where He went from being your Savior to being His Son, your Brother? Where He became I AM?

You've needed a Savior to bring you to where you are, but for the rest of the journey of your life you need to value the enormity that He is His Son. God sent a Savior, but brought home His Son. How have you missed it? How have all these years passed by and you've never understood the impact of the relationship?

You can't understand your inheritance, until you begin to grasp the enormity of I AM. The Spirit of Adoption in a child of God's life is the consciousness of what has been bequeathed to you, now and in eternity. What I AM really means. What you really have a hold of, what you truly possess. The Spirit of Adoption gives you the boldness and the confidence to cry "Abba Father" and to lay hold of your inheritance.

The Spirit of Might seized your wrist and catapulted you right into the Spirit of Truth where the manifested reality hit you of Who He was, of Who He is and Who He will become.

The Spirit of Adoption defines the embracing of your Brother as the accepting of the birthright. You, my friend, are a joint heir. And you have the same privileges as your Brother.

> ***Hebrews 2:11*** *(AMP)*
> *Both the One who makes men holy and those who are made holy are of the same family. So Jesus is not ashamed to call them **brothers**.*

(notice the common denominator of the family genetic code... holy)

The feeling of inferiority to receive your inheritance is what keeps us from using the gifts God has given us to produce fruit for the harvest, for the Kingdom of God.

The feeling of unworthiness is what makes you cling to a Savior and discount the capacity of The Son.

> ***John 15:16-17*** *(AMP)*
> *You have not chosen Me, but I have chosen you and I have appointed you (I have planted you), that you might go and bear fruit and keep on bearing and that*

your fruit may be lasting (that it may remain, abide), so that whatever you ask the Father in My Name (as presenting all that I AM) He may give it to you, this is what I command you; that you love one another.

John 14:13-13 (AMP)
And I will do (I Myself will grant) whatever you ask in My Name (as presenting all that I AM), so that the Father may be glorified and extolled in (through) the Son. (Yes) I will grant (I Myself will do for you) whatever you shall ask in My Name (as presenting all that I AM).

John 16:23 (AMP)
And when that time comes, you will ask nothing of Me (you will need to ask Me no questions), I assure you, most solemnly I tell you, that My Father will grant you whatever you ask in My Name (as presenting all that I AM). Up to this time you have not asked a (single) thing in My Name (as presenting all that I AM): but now ask and keep on asking

Matthew 21:22 (AMP)
And whatever you ask for in prayer, having faith and really believing you will receive.

It takes a giant leap of faith to ask in I AM's name. To dare tap into the Power of God with the boldness you can - because you invoke the name of I AM, whew, that is a trembling moment. This is behind the veil fruit. This is signs and wonders, the miraculous, the Power of God mentality that most of us won't ever dare to pursue. Don't get me wrong, there are legions that throw out "In the name of Jesus," with the wrong motive and with the wrong heart, and with the wrong level of maturity. The Spirit of Adoption is a different arena; **an arena marked by holy.** It is when you begin to understand I AM that is when you begin to understand your inheritance, but you can't understand I AM if you don't have a craving for Holy.

I AM heals. I AM delivers. I AM restores. I AM intercedes. I AM produces miracles. I AM produces signs and wonders.

In the arena of heaven, The I AMs are Hand in Hand producing the Power of God.

The Spirit of Adoption is what is pleading with you to hold out your hand, to grab hold of the prize of your inheritance. He's the One pointing out the fine points of the Will saying, "This is yours."

1 Corinthians 2:12 (AMP)
Now we have not received the spirit (that belongs to) the world, but the Holy Spirit Who is from God, (given to us) that we might realize and comprehend and appreciate the gifts (of divine favor and blessing so freely and lavishly) bestowed on us by God.

You don't know all you have the privilege to ask for if you don't understand I AM. The Spirit of Adoption requires that you believe. The Spirit of Adoption is where your faith begins. From the moment of your salvation to the desperate moments of your need, you can't believe if you can't comprehend I AM. With each level of your growth comes the realization of the magnitude of I AM. What comes, as wide-eyed awareness at your first breath, becomes steadfast resolution of truly who you are and where you are headed at your death.

He will give you what you need. That much is guaranteed in the Will -go ahead ask for it, but ask for it from I AM. I AM isn't just His title, I AM is your blood-bought inheritance.

If I AM has just been His title in your mind, imagine receiving a phone call from an attorney. He explains something incredible was left to you in the will of someone you desperately love. He would appreciate it if you could find the time to come to his office, so he could explain the details of your inheritance. How long would it take you to fit in his counsel? Something more powerful, more rewarding and more tangible than any earthly document has been bestowed on you. Don't you think it's time you learn, not hear but learn, what He left you? If you hear it, you'll forget it. If you learn it, you'll live it.

CHAPTER FOURTEEN

I sometimes wonder why on earth God chose me to do this project for Him, but I am convinced it's that spiritual principle... 'using what the world deems foolish to confuse the wise.'

Please don't let **'me'** get in the way of what God has revealed in this study. One day I was minding my own business, the next I was catapulted into something much bigger than I had any idea it would be. This isn't a book I've been able to write because I am more holy or more spiritual. Truthfully, seriously... ask my children, my husband, my parents, sisters, and my friends... I am so not. I am just their mom, wife, daughter, sister, and friend.

I pray from the depths of my soul that this book has intrigued you enough to go deeper and not just settle for the 'cliff notes' of the Spirit of God. But go into the deep where every time you pick up the Word, the Spirit of God envelops your heart, because you care enough to know more about Him. It happened in our Bible study over and over and over. You could ask the women that have been in the studies. We sometimes sat there stunned. Not at my feeble ability to communicate, but at the impact the Words of God had in our hearts. The center of our everything.

His Words severed like a laser and they cut right to the core of our beings, because we understood for the first time, in most of our lives, really what His Word said. It was so powerful, and I desperately desire it for you. Can you imagine the impact if the children of God really grasped what resides within them? Not the 'emotion' of what we have been taught, but the wisdom, understanding, knowledge, counsel, might, truth - all because we were adopted? Being able to tap into the Power of I AM, understanding the truth of what is available at our fingertips, because He's already given it to us? Unfortunately, we have only enough of the Word to be dangerous and we just aren't grown up enough yet to receive our inheritance. If we get it, I mean if we really get it, I am convinced there will be documents somewhere out there way in the future that state "Those were people who turned the world upside down!"

Instead of scaring the masses with our emotion, please, please for the love of our God let's lead them to Him. Let's explain it's so much more than a prayer. So much more than a ticket to eternity. So much more than hype and emotions. So much more than speaking in tongues, and so much more than a church service. HE is a precious, tangible God who loves them so much. HE is a God who is watching and waiting for just the right moment so He can breathe life into them, and seize them for eternity.

It puts it in a totally new framework. If we will unsear our hardened hearts and begin to pursue the things of the Spirit, not what we have believed for generations were the 'things of the Spirit,' but what God says are the 'things of the Spirit.' Here is the key to the study; we've pursued the gifts and the fruit, and we have never known what the 'things of the Spirit' are.

Things of the Spirit

Greek - aer

To breathe unconsciously

1. To blow
2. Air
3. Akin to a baffling wind

I hope you get the significance of that. If you don't, you probably might want to think about starting to read this book over again.

The **Things of the Spirit... to breathe, to blow, air...** *The Breath of God,* **The Anointing of God's Holy Spirit**. The Sevenfold Spirit of God breathed into man, the seven burning torches that represent the 'things' – The Spirit of Wisdom, The Spirit of Understanding, The Spirit of Counsel, The Spirit of Knowledge, The Spirit of Might, The Spirit of Truth and The Spirit of Adoption.

1 Peter 1:12 (AMP)
*The **things** of the Spirit above are the very things the angels long to look.*

TO LOOK in the Greek
The word is <u>parakupto</u>

It means the angels try to:

1. Peer into
2. Bend around
3. Lean over
4. Stoop to look into

Sure does sound to me like that is something **tangible** they are trying to see. Like a noun, like something that has form. Like a location. Seems like we've heard that somewhere before. God's Word is so awesome.

The Sevenfold Holy Spirit of God, the separated but single Godlikeness. One Sevenfold Spirit so close you can't tell where the beginning is or where the end is. Which is first and which is last. Which is Alpha or Omega or from vanishing point to vanishing point.

All things 'work together' for good takes on a brand new meaning.

Martin Luther described that Scripture like this...
*The Greek text has it the **singular** "works together" (sundergei), which is more fitting, since the **reference is to the Holy Spirit.***

'Works together'? ...the Sevenfold Spirit of God! So entwined, and so incredible, and all working together. How in the world have we missed this? Why have I spent most of my life focusing on the gifts of the Spirit and the fruit of the Spirit and not the Spirit of God Himself? Truthfully, I thought I had to wind up in all that 'stuff,' when you pursue the 'things' of the Spirit of God.

Sometimes I feel like my heart is going to explode. NO wonder. NO wonder He begs us to pursue wisdom first.

NO WONDER!

It's a huge revelation just waiting to happen!

God defines His Spirit over and over in the Word. He wants us to grasp, to comprehend His nature, the separated but single Godlikeness of His Spirit.

THE SEVENFOLD ONE HOLY SPIRIT OF GOD

The Spirit of Wisdom
– *He will woo you.*

The Spirit of Understanding
– *He will consume you.*

The Spirit of Knowledge
– *He will reveal to you.*

The Spirit of Counsel
– *He will speak to you.*

The Spirit of Might
– *He will empower you.*

The Spirit of Truth
– *He will testify to you.*

The Spirit of Adoption
– *He will birth and retrieve you.*

THE DOUBLE PORTION ANOINTING?

The Spirit of Wisdom
 – *He wants intimacy with you.*

The Spirit of Understanding
 – *He wants you to crave Him.*

The Spirit of Knowledge
 – *He wants you to know Him deeply.*

The Spirit of Counsel
 – *He wants you to hear Him*

The Spirit of Might
 – *He wants you to trust Him.*

The Spirit of Truth
 – *He wants you to understand Him.*

The Spirit of Adoption
 – *He wants you to know you are His.*

CHAPTER FIFTEEN

I have asked myself over and over, why does it really matter? Why has God decided to penetrate this so deeply into my spirit? I will never know exactly why, but I have a deep sense it's because of where I was and what I went through.

I know I am not the only one out there. I know I'm not the only one who watches from a distance as people are blown on and then they fall over, "Is that God's Spirit? Is that truly the job of His Spirit in this day? "

The emotionalism of the '21st century Holy Spirit' baffles me. Our culture has turned the intimate, personal, private matter of our union with God into a sideshow. If it hurts me, how does it make Him feel?

I could go on here, we all could, but to just maybe open some eyes is good enough for me. I have never had anything impact my walk with the Lord more dramatically than what happened when the 'Holy Spirit' abuse began to affect my life. When I had to believe it was 'God' because I was told it was God, and I didn't know how to fight it.

This tiny voice down deep inside kept fighting its way to the top. It wasn't until my world crumbled that I listened enough to hear "it's in the Word, now get in there."

My answer, my peace, my understanding finally came. I dove as deep as my tiny mind would allow into a Book, the very Words of God.

God has settled this issue once and for all in my life. I am no longer moved by man's interpretation of the Holy Spirit's destiny for my life. I listen to only one interpretation, and it is on the pages of a Book I keep very, very close beside me. I pay attention to only one Voice, and it is the one that finally rescued me from my pit.

During my ordeal I once had a 'pastor' demand, "Married women can't hear directly from God, they have to hear from God through their husbands." I wonder how irritated the Lord feels about that statement. I wonder how this 'pastor' can back that up scripturally. I wonder how many in his congregation believe him, and will never, ever have a precious intimate encounter with the Son who died for them, a God who planned for them, and a Spirit that consumes them.

It's taken me a long time to get to this point, but now I pity him. He is as confused as I was. He doesn't understand the truth about the Holy Spirit of God.

The Holy Spirit isn't just for men or for women. It isn't just for the 'more anointed' or the 'more persecuted.'

The Holy Spirit has one job, and that is to bring home God's family. That is a huge requirement and an enormous undertaking.

God breathes into any person regardless of sex, age or circumstance who says, "I believe; I believe in a Son named Jesus, and what He did on that cross, He did for me."

They don't have to understand obedience, they don't have to understand repentance means turning away from, and they don't have to understand one single principle out of the Word of God to qualify for the Breath of God to be blown into their spirit. They just have to believe and breathe.

Once they breathe in, they are forever hereditarily altered. It is then the Holy Spirit of God's vocation to bring home His child.

OK, so let's start with me. Let's go back. I'm not afraid to say I was deceived, I was wrong, I just flat out missed the mark. Please don't you be.

God is giving us another chance. A chance to change and show a hurting, suffering world there is an answer. Our suffering world is scared to death of our spastic, frenzied outpouring of 'This Spirit' that we call God.

The emotionalism and the false doctrine we have portrayed for the last decade is just that - emotion and lies. We have the Spirit of God dwelling inside us. He is there for a reason. Emotion isn't it. **It is to make us holy**.

The emotionalism of the service won't keep you holy to the parking lot. The deep realization of what dwells in every tiny corpuscle of your being will give you one profound sense of reverence. After all, it's His greatest work to make us holy, and it's His deepest desire to do so.

Holy does have a place, and in your life right now, can you say that He's in it?

Most of the time life seems to push the most important moment of our existence to the very recesses of our being – the moment we breathed in our God.

It doesn't happen intentionally; it just happens. But when we begin to breathe in a fresh breath of His Spirit, when we begin to pursue the 'things of the Spirit,' that's when we realize what we have been missing. The void, the emptiness inside comes from a lack of awareness of what has possessed us. A lack of awareness of what is touching, hearing and feeling every move, and every word we speak. A lack of awareness we are being closely watched.

He's there, whether you want to acknowledge Him or not. If you said "I believe" and you meant it, He's there. You may not feel it, you may not want to believe it, but it doesn't change the veracity.

His Spirit has intermingled with your soul, and there is just no getting out of it. His Spirit is what has you reading this book. His Spirit is what is pounding on the inner sanctum of your head saying, "I'm here."

For some of you, you have been terrified you have to act like the 'emotionalist Holy Spirit people' to ever feel the Touch of God or to ever hear the Voice of God. If that is what it means to be spirit-filled, no thank you. But that's not true.

You don't have to laugh uncontrollably, you don't have to run down the aisles, and you don't have to pass out in the pew. Heck, you don't even have to act like you are being shocked with electricity when you feel the presence of God. You don't have to pursue the prophetic, and you absolutely don't have to speak in tongues to understand the Holy Spirit.

In fact He prefers that you prioritize. He prefers you get in the Word and pursue Him. Seek Wisdom first.

If there is gut-wrenching emotion let it be private. Remember, the Spirit of Knowledge is a personal, private matter. It's intimate, it's cleansing and it's incredible. It's a joy you will never understand unless you have experienced it. It's a peace that passes all understanding; it's a love you haven't ever felt even from the greatest love of your life. It's a tender, passionate, consuming encounter with the Spirit of the Living God, and 'the encounter' has an agenda. That is to change you to be more like Him. And that, my friend, is Holy. You need to remember His name, The Holy Spirit.

Father, Son and Spirit are bringing home their children, and they reside in Holy. Pursue Wisdom first, and at the Throne you will be allowed to understand what that Holy feels like. You will begin to crave Holy. And you will embark on doing anything you can to pursue it.

FINAL THOUGHTS

The last words Christ spoke to His disciples right before His crucifixion were "Peace I leave to you. Peace, not as the world knows, but My peace I leave to you." I can't tell you how that one sentence has so desperately changed my life. How I went from borderline destruction to better than I have ever been.

There is a Scripture we ignore most of the time, "Pursue peace, go after it." When I started to apply that, when I began to heal, it changed every relationship, every circumstance that I had. It didn't matter if I was right anymore, it didn't even matter if they were wrong. All that mattered was I needed peace, and I was willing to 'settle' to receive it.

I finally realized my pride was killing me. Literally, it was killing me. In the scope of things, who cares if Lori is right, really? The only one is Lori, and she is doing herself in. I don't debate anymore what I believe. I don't cling to the fact I need to prove what I say. I am believing you will receive this book as just that. Not an attempt on my part to 'prove I am right.' Not even an attempt to change your mind, but maybe to just open your eyes to something you haven't been taught.

I needed a God who would just hold me in His arms. One who would hold me and say "I know, I know" like my parents used to do. I just needed someone who could see it 'all' and could discern right from wrong to comfort me. I was a big part of the wrong, but from my perspective I couldn't see it. I didn't need any more conviction, any more brow beatings, any more manipulation. I just needed someone who understood to hold me.

What I got caught up in for a year and a half was so much bigger than anybody involved really understood at the time. There was a turning point for me, right around the middle of December several years ago.

I remember being alone in my bed so sad - my dad was

so ill, my husband was still missing and my heart was so, so broken. I remember a touch, and then an embrace. A precious God who didn't need to qualify the right or the wrong, who didn't need to make me understand where He stood. He just wanted to hold me. And He wanted to rock.

The methodic rocking felt like I was nestled tightly in His lap, wrapped snuggly in His arms and it began to sound more and more like "Peace, peace, you need peace."

When I would try to tell Him what had happened, like a child through broken sobs, all I could hear was "Sssh, ssssh, ssssh, I already know, I already know." I didn't even have to say I was sorry; He already knew.

When your embrace has been able to quell the heartbrokenness of your child, it's then they will listen.

He firmly spoke to my heart, "Child, pursue peace, go after it. It is peace that I left to you, I said it last so you would remember... Peace, Lori, peace." He said, "My Word is your answer," and then my mind flashed to his scarred wrists, and it hit me. My emotional scars were nothing, absolutely nothing. What He placed in my lap I will never, ever 'not remember.' He strategically placed a Book, one He meticulously maintains, and He smiled and said, "Lori, don't you ever, ever forget it."

Peace, peace, my friend. I pray that you will find peace. Not as the world defines peace, but the peace of the I AM, ...who wants to rock.